SPOKANE

Pictorial Research by David Reynolds
"Partners in Progress" by John Shideler

Produced in Cooperation with the
Spokane Historic Preservation Foundation

Windsor Publications, Inc.
Northridge, California

A VIEW OF THE FALLS

An Illustrated History Of

SPOKANE

WILLIAM STIMSON

Windsor Publications, Inc.—History Book Division

Publisher: John M. Phillips
Editorial Director: Teri Davis Greenberg

Staff for *A View of the Falls*
Design Director: Alexander D'Anca
Senior Editor: Pamela Schroeder
Picture Editor: Julie Jaskol
Director, Corporate Biographies: Karen Story
Assistant Director, Corporate Biographies: Phyllis Gray
Editor, Corporate Biographies: Judith Hunter
Editorial Assistants: Kathy M. Brown, Tricia Cobb, Lonnie Pham, Patricia Pittman
Design and Layout: Christina McKibbin

Library of Congress Cataloging in Publication Data
Stimson, William, 1946-
A view of the falls.

"Produced in cooperation with the Spokane Historic Preservation Foundation."
Bibliography: p. 154
Includes index.
1. Spokane (Wash.)—History. 2. Spokane (Wash.)—Description. 3. Spokane (Wash.)—Industries.
I. Reynolds, David (David B.) II. Spokane Historic Preservation Foundation. III. Title.
F899.S7S78 1985 979.7'37 85-9276
ISBN 0-89781-121-6

Published 1985
Printed in the United States of America
First Edition

Honorary Advisors
Windsor Publications and the Spokane Historic Preservation Foundation wish to acknowledge the following individuals, who lent valuable assistance in the preparation of this volume:
Jay Kent Adams
James E. Chase
Gerald Hester
David M. Peterson
Jack Sloane
Michael Wilson

Page two: *The Jesuits of the Mission of the Sacred Heart, near the Coeur d'Alene River, sought to convert the Spokane and Coeur d'Alene Indians. Courtesy, Eastern Washington State Historical Society (EWSHS)*

Contents

I

•The Land As Fate•

Facing page: *The thundering Spokane falls convinced James Glover he had found the site for a new town. In this view, taken in May 1889, a few weeks before the Spokane fire, the first Howard Street Bridge can be seen, upper right, crossing the main falls of the Spokane River. The bridge was wooden, and did not survive the fire. Courtesy, (EWSHS)*

Spokane's history begins deep in the earth, where the heat generated by the downward pressure of the earth's gravity creates immense caldrons of molten rock. When this magma—as the liquid rock is called—finds an avenue upward, it generally becomes trapped under the crust of the earth and creates a bulge—a mountain. The mountains north and east of Spokane were created by such forces hundreds of millions of years ago.

As the magma at the center of these newly created mountains cooled, it shriveled and cracked, leaving fissures like pipelines running to every part of the mountain. Super-heated water came boiling up from the core of the earth through these fissures, bringing with it dissolved gold, silver, lead, zinc and other minerals. Millions of years of such activity laced the mountains of this region with the riches that would one day re-direct Spokane history.

But it was magma that did not stop below the earth's surface that created most of what we see. Some 15 million years ago, in an event unique to geological history, cracks in the earth's surface ranging in size from a few feet to a few yards began opening up in what is now southeastern Washington and northeastern Oregon. Out of these fissures flowed oceans of syrupy molten rock in volumes sufficient to travel, in some cases, hundreds of miles. When it was all over, most of Eastern Washington and large sections of Oregon and Idaho were covered with the reddish-brown basalt a mile thick on the average. All the land in the vicinity of Spokane stood at the level of Five Mile Prairie and the South Hill. Then the river began to chisel itself a new channel, creating after 12 million years of work, the Spokane Valley.

Sometimes the river found a layer of basalt more resistant than usual. It passed over this rock and continued its drilling beyond, leaving a shelf for the water to spill over. This is how the Spokane falls was created. Meanwhile the prevailing southwest winds were dusting the basalt with a rich silt, laying down, bit by bit, the dune-like hills of the Palouse. Going back millions of years, but as recently as 1980, the volcanos to the west periodically exploded and contributed wind-borne minerals which make the Palouse soil extraordinary.

Long after the lava flows, just 10,000 to 15,000 years ago, the region was altered by another, more sudden, cataclysm. A cooling in the earth's climate created many immense glaciers in this area. One of these huge accumulations of ice blocked a canyon and stopped the flow of Montana's Clark Fork River into the Pend Oreille Lake. The river water backed up for dozens of years and filled three long canyons covering much of western Montana.

Suddenly the glacier holding back all this water gave way. The result was the greatest flood ever to occur on earth. An estimated 500 cubic miles of water surged down the Rathdrum valley, across the area of Spokane and down the center of Washington State.

As a strong stream from a garden hose plucks out and carries pebbles with it, so this deluge carried rocks and boulders it

Basalt chutes line the old Sunset Highway, west of Spokane. An ocean of lava once covered the Inland Empire. When it cooled it cracked vertically, leaving the pillar-like designs where humans or nature cut through it. (EWSHS)

had collected on its route. Some of the material built up dams across small valleys east of Spokane, causing the water of their streams to accumulate. This created a whole series of lakes, including Coeur d'Alene, Hayden, Liberty, and Newman. Other rocks brought by the flood settled in the Rathdrum and Spokane valley floors. Covered over eventually by a layer of soil, these rocks formed the filter-like underground stream or "aquifer" from which the city of Spokane would get its water.

It happened that the area of present Spokane was already covered by an immense glacial lake when this deluge struck, so its features were cushioned from the violence. The higher land southwest of the city had no such protection, and the floodwaters splashed upon it like a bucket of water upon a dusty sidewalk. The soil was scrubbed away, leaving behind Eastern Washington's sculpturesque but nearly barren "scablands." The turbulence of the water was such that it even plucked out basalt in places, creating the basins of the lakes south and west of Spokane.

We do not know if human beings were present to witness—or perhaps be swept away by—this colossal flood. But man was at least nearby. It was about the time of the last of the floods, about 10,000 years ago, that the young man found in the Marmes burial site (named for the modern-day owner of the land) was buried in a canyon about fifty miles west of Pullman. It could not have been long, given the nomadic ways of such tribes, before similar groups lived in the Spokane area.

Virtually nothing is known about the progress of the Indians from the time of their Ice Age arrival to the time when whites discovered them inhabiting this area. Through their own Pasteurs and Edisons, however, they had triumphed over their environment. Instead of shivering against the cold under a pile of brush, as his ancestors had, the modern Indian had learned to live in a snug cone-shaped shelter, large enough to allow comfort, small enough to be kept warm by a small fire. Instead of foraging daily for scraps of food to keep him alive, he had become so efficient at gathering and preserving foods that he could go through a harsh winter without stirring from his tent if he didn't care to. His style of life was pleasant and secure. On the whole, the common-rank Spokane Indian of, say, 1500 A.D. was in all probability safer, healthier, and better fed than his European counterpart.

These pictographs were painted by the Spokane Indians on a cave wall near the Little Spokane River (shown here as they appeared in 1920). Today the earth-colored paintings are nearly obliterated by vandalism. Although many such drawings have been found throughout the Northwest, the meaning of the designs is not known. (EWSHS)

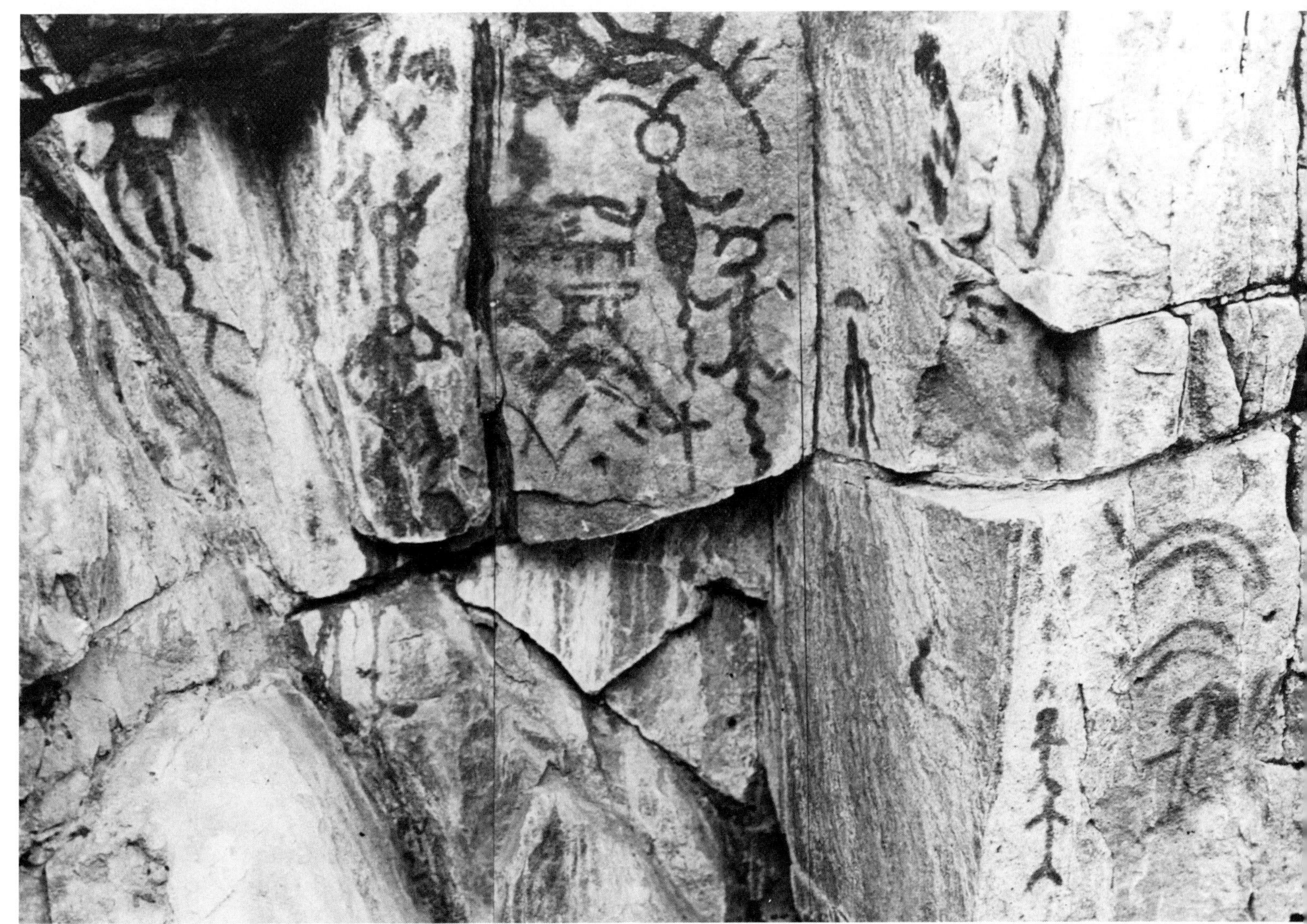

In the 1870s more than 3,000 Spokanes lived in small villages scattered across the area. The name "Spokanee" means "Children of the Sun," and refers to the three Spokane tribes. The upper tribe was located near Lake Coeur d'Alene, the middle around what is now Spokane, and the lower tribe camped at the mouth of the Spokane River. (EWSHS)

What the Indians had discovered over the thousands of years, while Europeans experimented with agriculture, was that the land, if one knew how to use it, would easily support a small population. Locating, harvesting, and preserving fruits, seeds, herbs, trees, bark, leaves, and mushrooms constituted a virtual botanical science—and one that had to be mastered by each Indian family. Modern botanists have discovered at least 200 natural growing products used by the Indians of this area. Soapberries, for example, are bitter; but placed in a bowl with a few wild strawberries for sweetening and whipped, they became a tasty pink froth called "Indian ice cream" that was served to guests. A tea made from the same bush was used as a medicine for an upset stomach. The leaves, when boiled, produced a popular shampoo.

Gathering these products through the year was pleasant and varied employment. In early spring when the snow was gone an Indian village of several hundred people would dismantle its winter camp (which was usually near a river) and divide up into small family groups. Each would go into its own traditional fields to begin the harvest of spring plants.

The whole tribe, and often members from other tribes, would gather again in June by the river to fish for salmon. Spawning salmon once swam all the way to the Spokane falls, and catching them there with spears and nets, then cleaning and drying them for storage, was a major industry that employed hundreds, all taking orders from a "salmon chief."

When the salmon season was over the Indians would strike their tents and move to the damp meadows to gather

The annual return of the salmon to the Spokane falls inspired an Indian celebration. Each summer well-organized groups gathered at prime locations up and down the riverbanks to spear spawners. Construction of mammoth hydro-electric dams on the Spokane and Columbia rivers ended the salmon runs in the 1930s. (EWSHS)

camas, a root that was baked and eaten as bread. When autumn came the Indians once again scattered in smaller groups to go to the hills to pick berries. Families went to the same gullies and clearings year after year, and so took care of them as they would their own farms. They never over-harvested and they employed many techniques for keeping the bushes productive—they knew, for example, that breaking a huckleberry stem at just the right place would make two berries grow instead of one the next season.

In the fall and winter the men hunted deer, bear, and other game. The hunt of buffalo, an animal which existed in large numbers only east of the Rocky Mountains, provided the Spokanes and Coeur d'Alenes with their annual adventure into Blackfeet country, where all intruders were attacked as a matter of policy. Except for these forays, the Spokanes, Coeur d'Alenes and other small tribes of this immediate area were different from most Indian tribes—and most human civilizations—in that they lived virtually without war. Their dealings with other tribes were in the form of trade. The Spokanes and Coeur d'Alenes served as middlemen, trading dried salmon for buffalo hides with the Blackfeet, then trading the hides for shells, wood carvings and other products of the coastal Indians.

Early in the nineteenth century Euro-

Right: *Father Joseph Joset, S.J., shown here in 1870, was priest to the Coeur d'Alene Indians, and with fellow Jesuits, founder of the Mission of the Sacred Heart. Joset was instrumental in arranging a temporary cease-fire between the tribes and Colonel Edward Steptoe's dragoons during the latter's retreat. Later, during Colonel George Wright's punitive action, Joset was able to secure more lenient conditions for the Coeur d'Alenes. (EWSHS)*

Right: *Listed in the National Register of Historic Places, Cataldo Mission is the oldest known standing building in the state of Idaho. Shown here in the 1920s, the mission has been reconstructed several times since 1928. (EWSHS)*

pean men took to decorating themselves with hats made of beaver furs. Meeting the demand for the pelts of these little animals was the enterprise that brought white civilization among the Northwest Indians. In 1810 the North West Company, a Canadian firm, established the first of several trading posts that would operate where the Spokane River meets the Little Spokane River.

The first missionaries to the area, the Reverends Elkanah Walker and Cushing Eells, arrived with their wives in 1838 and built a small mission on the Walla Walla-Colville Road, near what is now Ford, Washington. The accommodating Indians converted in large numbers and then went on living more or less as they always had. "We have been here almost nine years," Mrs. Eells admitted to her diary, "and have not been permitted to hear the cries of one penitent, or the songs of one redeemed soul." Later missionaries, notably the trusted Reverend Henry T. Cowley and the tireless Jesuits Pierre De Smet, Joseph Joset and Joseph Cataldo, would do better by taking the time to learn the Indians' way of life and meeting them half way.

Over a period of four decades, the Indians gradually became accustomed to the whites. From the traders they were happy to acquire guns, factory-made knives, traps, and tobacco. From the missionaries they took a little Christianity without, as Mrs. Eells lamented, altering their lives unduly. Among the diaries, letters, and memoirs of the time, it's hard to find a white with much bad to say of the Spokanes and Coeur d'Alenes. Where they are recorded on the subject, the Indians professed to find the whites friendly and reliable.

But inevitably there would come a crisis. The Willamette Valley not so far to the south was the termination point of the Oregon Trail. By the 1850s the Willamette and adjacent valleys were already beginning to fill up with homesteaders and miners. The white culture, instead of being an aspect of life in the region, was swiftly becoming life itself. The Indians of the Northwest were in good communication, and all the tribes to the north heard what was happening to the Indians of the Willamette Valley as whites came. One entire tribe, the Klikitats, had been removed by the U.S. Army to Yakima country. No tribe could remain impassive in the face of such stories. Some renegades in what is now central Oregon had already commenced guerrilla warfare by indiscriminately attacking wagon trains, miners, and other white targets.

In 1853, Isaac I. Stevens was given the dual title of governor of Washington Territory (the territory's first) and Superintendent of Indian Affairs for the new territory. His most important assignment was to make the area safe for settlement by winning treaties with the Indians.

Stevens had the kind of brilliance and

Left: *Located twenty-five miles northeast of Spokane at Ford, Tshimakain (Chemakane) was the first Protestant mission in northeastern Washington. This lithograph was drawn by J.M. Stanley in 1853, about four years after the Reverends Elkanah Walker and Cushing Eells had closed the mission. Stanley accompanied Isaac Stevens on his expedition across the territory and his drawings provided Congress with their first pictures of the Pacific Northwest. (EWSHS)*

Right: *Governor Isaac Stevens was appointed first territorial governor of Washington in 1853. Stevens' major tasks were to organize a civil government in the territory and treat with the Indian tribes. He was elected a delegate to Congress from the territory in 1857 and was killed in the Civil War a few years later. (EWSHS)*

Far right: *Hudson's Bay Company sent Spokane Garry to Fort Garry (now Winnipeg, Manitoba) in 1825. He learned to read, write, and speak English, and was converted to Christianity. Five years later he returned as the first Protestant missionary to the Spokane Indians. Garry also built the first school in Spokane and became its first teacher. (EWSHS)*

ambition that could put a person out of sync with the rest of the human race. He had graduated first in his West Point class and then had plunged into a series of army assignments with such vigor and imagination that it alternately thrilled and outraged superiors. Within a year of his appointment he had concluded treaties with most of the coastal tribes. A few months later, on May 29, 1855, he had representatives of many interior tribes assembled at a council at Walla Walla. The Spokanes and Coeur d'Alenes were not involved in these negotiations but, knowing they would be next to deal with Stevens, they sent Chief Spokane Garry to observe.

Stevens, always impatient and decisive, had already drawn on a map the reservations that were to be offered. Wagons, blankets and other inducements were to be thrown into the deal. But he insisted the treaties be signed there and then. The Indians signed. But many of them were dissatisfied with the size and locations of their assigned reservations. Instead of instruments of peace, Stevens' treaties became a focus of resentment among most Indians. If Stevens had not already realized this, it was made clear to him by the Spokanes when he visited them in December of 1855. "I had there," Stevens recalled later in his meticulous record of the meetings, "one of the most stormy councils for three days that had ever occurred in my whole Indian experience."

One chief after another rose to say that he did not want war, but Stevens' own behavior at the Walla Walla council was making it difficult to argue for peace. Spokane Garry chided Stevens for his high-handed attitude toward Indians:

When you look at the red men, you think you have more heart, more sense, than these poor Indians. I think the difference between us and you Americans is in the clothing: the blood and body are the same. Do you think, because your mother was white and their's dark, that you are higher or better? We are dark, yet if we cut ourselves, the blood will be red, and with the whites it is the same, though their skin is white. I do not think we are poor because we belong to another nation. If you take those Indians for men, treat them so now.

Chiefs of both the Spokane and Coeur d'Alene tribes made two things clear to Stevens. The first was that they had no intention of joining the other tribes in the area which were even then making war against the whites. The second was that, until there was a treaty, whites must respect Indian borders.

The army, which in these years frequently had more sympathy for the Indian side than that of the whites, knew that Stevens' treaties were causing the problem. Colonel Edward Steptoe, commander of the fort at Walla Walla, told his superiors that in his opinion enforcing the treaties, "will be followed by immediate hostilities with most of the tribes in this part of the country; for which reason it does appear to me greatly desirable that a new commission be appointed, and a new treaty made, thoroughly digested and accepted by both sides."

Meanwhile, Kamiakin, a chief of the Yakimas and leader of the Indian resistance, came among the Spokanes and Coeur d'Alenes to try to persuade them to join the war. Many important chiefs, including Garry of the Spokanes and Victor of the Coeur d'Alenes, argued for peace. But the call of Kamiakin for Indians to stand together now or die was persuasive to many others. Kamiakin was arguing that eventually white soldiers would come and force the Spokanes and Coeur d'Alenes into exile.

Then, on May 6, 1858, Colonel Steptoe decided to take four companies of cavalry from Walla Walla to Colville to assess the fears of some white settlers who felt they were in danger from Indians. Knowing of the friendly relations between the whites and Indians of this region, Steptoe was skeptical of the reports of imminent uprisings. But about halfway on through his journey, in the rolling hills of the grass-covered Palouse hills (north of the present Colfax), he was surprised to look up and find the crests of the hills lined with Indians in war regalia. Steptoe met with the chiefs and assured them he meant them no harm. They apparently accepted his word, but some excited braves had begun to taunt the soldiers. Some shots were fired. In defending themselves the soldiers soon killed a chief of the Coeur d'Alenes and several other Indians, causing the Indian mood to turn from

As whites expanded the township of Spokane Falls, the main Spokane tribe moved further west to where Latah (Hangman) Creek empties into the river. Teepees could still be seen in that area, known as Indian Canyon, up to the 1920s. These Spokanes were camped in Peaceful Valley, west of the Spokane River falls, circa 1880. (EWSHS)

cockiness to hot anger. After a two-day running battle (May 16 and 17) Steptoe led his men to the refuge of a hill. As night fell, the whole command of 156—two company officers had already fallen—was surrounded by approximately 1,000 Indians. Then it was discovered that so little ammunition had been packed that each of Steptoe's soldiers had only about four rounds left. It looked as if the command would be easily overwhelmed come morning. But in the dark of the night Steptoe and his men managed the now famous escape through the lines of the sleeping Indians.

What an irony that Steptoe, who, like many army officers at the time, sympathized with the Indian cause, and the Spokanes and Coeur d'Alenes, the most peaceable tribes in the territory, should have ended up destroying each other in this accidental and meaningless little battle. Steptoe, whose health had been fragile already, never recovered from the rigorous march of escape and soon retired from the army, a virtual invalid. The Spokanes and Coeur d'Alenes would always mark this two days of battle as the opening of an era of endless heartbreak.

The Jesuits who lived among the Coeur d'Alenes tried to mediate before there was more violence. But it was too late for amicable solutions. Three months later, Colonel George Wright rode out the gate of Fort Walla Walla at the head of a force of 570 regulars and 30 Nez Perce scouts, heading north to get revenge.

On August 31, 1858, Wright's troops made their camp at Basset Spring, halfway between the present towns of Medical Lake and Cheney. The following morning the soldiers awoke to find a group of Indians at the top of a hill two miles to the north. Wright eagerly deployed his troops in two sections, like a two-handed grab at the hill, but the Indians fled down the far side. When Wright and his officers reached the crest of the hill they saw hundreds of Indians below. On order, the well-drilled infantry pressed down upon the Indian formation until it shattered into fleeing individuals. At that moment, the dragoons, who had been leading their horses at a walk behind the infantry, mounted and galloped after the Indians. Lieutenant Lawrence Kip, who was watching with Wright from the top of the hill, said in his diary: "We saw the flash of their sabers as they cut them down. Lt. Davidson shot one warrior from his saddle as they charged up, and Lt. Gregg clove the skull of another. Yells and shrieks and uplifted hands were of no avail as they rode over them."

A few days later the Spokanes again threw themselves in front of Wright's advance, using the distraction of grass fires (on land now occupied by Fairchild Air Force Base) to get closer to the soldiers. But Wright quickly analyzed the danger and ordered his troops to attack through the flames. This "Battle of Spokane Plains," like the previous "Battle of Four Lakes," hardly deserved the distinction of a name. In the whole campaign Wright's only battle casualty was one wounded man. The Indians' campfire enthusiasm and dash-in-and-shoot tactics were no match for those who made a profession and science of war.

While he was camped on a bluff overlooking the Spokane River (a site which forty years later would be occupied by Fort George Wright), Wright received word that Chief Spokane Garry wanted to talk. The two met on the river bank, near where the Mission Street Bridge is now. Wright told Garry that if the Indians wanted peace, "You must come with your arms, with your women and children, and everything you have, and lay them at my feet; you must put your faith in me and trust to my mercy." Otherwise, Wright said, he would "exterminate" the tribe. This was the very word he used.

Living in permanent dwellings, wearing white people's clothing, and cultivating crops, these Spokane Indian children at the Spokane reservation circa 1900 were forced to adopt a way of life that was previously unknown to their people. (EWSHS)

Garry took Wright's terms back to the Spokanes while Wright turned east, toward the territory of the Coeur d'Alene Indians. The soldiers happened to capture a herd of 800 Indian horses near what is now the Idaho border. Horses were both the wealth and the war machines of the Indians. Unable to take them with him, Wright assigned two companies to slaughter them.

When Wright arrived in Coeur d'Alene country, that tribe immediately sued for peace. The colonel demanded total subjugation, took some prisoners, and returned eastward to accept the surrender of the Spokane tribe. The Spokanes surrendered on a site twenty miles to the southwest of the Spokane Falls, at a creek then called Latah.

Later that same day, September 24, 1855, Chief Owhi of the Yakimas rode in and gave himself up. Wright had him put in irons and sent word to Owhi's son, a notorious killer of whites called Qualchan, that the father would be hanged if Qualchan did not also surrender immediately. Qualchan did come in the next morning, but apparently without having gotten Wright's message, because he acted surprised when he heard his father was already there. Why Qualchan came in, under a white flag, no one will ever know, because Wright had him dragged to a tree and hanged within minutes of his arrival. The following day, a large party of Palouse Indians came to the camp to surrender. Six of them were also hanged from nearby trees, and the stream that flows by the place has ever after been known as Hangman Creek in Wright's dubious honor.

The Spokanes, Coeur d'Alenes and other tribes of eastern Washington never again warred against whites. After they

Spokane Indian Joe Robinson roasts meat the traditional way in 1900 in Indian Canyon. As the Indians were forced onto the reservations, much of their culture was diluted by white society. A handful of Spokanes, however, have taken an active part in preserving the language, arts, and traditions that were practiced by their people for hundreds of years. (EWSHS)

recovered from the loss of horses and food stores routinely destroyed by Wright's men, life for the Indians of the area returned almost to normal.

But twenty years later, all the things that had been foretold to the Indians, which had caused them to confront Steptoe's troops, suddenly came to pass. The railroads were approaching.

Father Alexander Diomedi, a Jesuit who had been working among the Coeur d'Alenes, called the men of that tribe together and warned them that whites would soon be so numerous that the fish, the game, and the prairies would disappear. If the Indians did not consent to go to a reservation and take up farming, Diomedi told them, "your children will starve; your wives and daughters will be unsafe; you yourselves will disappear."

The Indians were stunned. Finally, one by the name of Alexander stood and said they had never required much to live and would not when the whites arrived. "You need bread, we have camas; you require good clothing, we are satisfied with deer skins and buffalo robes. We can live comfortably on what you think poor and wretched." Surely, Alexander thought, these few things would still be available to Indians after the whites came. They were finally persuaded otherwise by Diomedi, however, and the Coeur d'Alene tribe removed to its reservation in 1878.

The Spokane tribe reacted differently. It had to learn the hard way. The reservation for the Spokanes was established in 1881 (the same year the city of Spokane was incorporated and the first railroad reached it). But many Spokanes refused to sign a treaty and go there. Members of the tribe began picking out pieces of land around the city, prepared to live alongside the white man in the white man way. Some became good farmers and horse ranchers, but one by one all were pushed off their property. Timothy Brooks, one of the first white settlers near Deep Creek, southwest of Spokane, admitted that he himself had taken land occupied by Indians. Looking back in a 1925 interview Brooks said:

None of us in those days thought that an Indian had any rights that a white man was bound to respect. The Indians didn't know anything about the homestead laws and regulations and no one was anxious to put them wise. There were always little technicalities which one could raise against an Indian's claim with a good prospect of winning out against the Indian in the land office, in case he showed fight and persisted in trying to hang on to the land he wanted. Looking back, it is quite possible that we weren't always quite fair to those Indians.

The tragedy of the Indians is suggested by the story of Garry. Despite his blunt talk to Stevens, Garry had always believed that whites and Indians would learn to live together peaceably. As a young boy he had been educated by whites (thus his Anglicized name) and taught Christianity to his fellow tribe members. He refused to go to war against Colonel Wright, even though his pacifism probably meant he would be killed by the Indians had they won.

In the 1870s he was forced off two different ranches by white settlers. He then settled with a small band of followers in Hangman Creek, but was harassed by rowdies from town. Garry's daughter Nellie approached Garvin Mouat, a homesteader whose land included what is now Indian Canyon Golf Course, and asked if the small band could pitch their tepees on his land. Mouat consented and consequently got to know Garry in the last years of his life.

"Garry's wife was blind," Mouat recalled many years later, "and Garry used to take care of her. He would lift her on and off the horse, and for riding would tie her on the horse and lead the horse. He was very attentive to her. After Garry died I went into his tepee, where Garry's body was lying stretched out on an old bedtick and Garry's old wife, her face like parchment and her hands on his chest, was kneeling by his remains moaning." Garry is buried in Greenwood Cemetery, a short distance from where he spent the final years of his life.

By 1887 the Spokanes had seen the futility of trying to hold onto any of this land and consented to move down the river to the reservation. Twenty years later, Spokane historian William S. Lewis talked to seven Spokane chiefs and found them still troubled. Speaking through an interpreter, they said they had never received the farming equipment and cash payments they were promised to help them establish on the new land: "When we were driven from our lands we left our farms, our gardens, our hunting grounds, our fishing places, and the burial places of our fathers. When we were compelled to move onto the reservation it was like putting birds in a cage. All the time since we have been waiting for some white men to come and tell us what to do."

What to do was the problem. Everything the Indian thought, did or valued depended on his owning this land, and this land was lost to him.

But at the same time it was opened to others. Tens of thousands of people—in the eastern part of the United States, in Ireland, England, France, Germany and Italy, and even as far away as China—were hearing about the American West and beginning to dream of tying their own fates to it.

II

• THE CITY BUILDERS •

Facing page: *Workers construct the first Northern Pacific warehouse in 1883 on Railroad Avenue, between Lincoln and Post streets. In 1881 Railroad Avenue was created as the thoroughfare for the railway lines between First and Second avenues. The tracks on Railroad Avenue were elevated to their present level in 1915, so traffic could move more smoothly on the downtown north-to-south streets. (EWSHS)*

With the end of the Civil War in 1865 the move west had begun in earnest. The Willamette Valley, at the termination of the Oregon Trail, filled quickly and settlers pushed on to adjacent valleys, including the Yakima Valley. From Yakima the migration gravitated steadily north. At first settlers in the Palouse country stayed in the lowlands along streams, thinking the hills unsuitable for agriculture. But latecomers with little choice gave the hills a try and, after a season or two of struggle against the tough bunch grass sod, produced an excellent crop of wheat. It became axiomatic among farmers with some experience that wheat would grow anywhere there was bunch grass, and bunch grass was everywhere in this country.

A second kind of migration, one of miners, simultaneously began to push into the mountains of Spokane country. The first important gold strikes were made in the Okanogan to the north in 1874 and in the Coeur d'Alene to the east in 1878.

The first settlers and miners could replenish their supplies as they passed through old established military towns like Walla Walla and Colville. But when they found their homesteading and mining sites and went to work, they would need close-by places to buy their nails, flour, coffee and other provisions. This gave rise to a third category of Western pioneer: the city builder. Mining towns like Molson in the Okanogan and Burke in the Coeur d'Alene appeared overnight, and generally were abandoned just as quickly when the quality of the ore slipped (which is why today's ghost towns were virtually all originally mining towns). Farming towns—Rosalia, Colfax, Ritzville, Spangle, and many others still on the map—appeared wherever a couple of dozen farmers found they were more than a full day's round-trip ride to the next town.

The shopkeepers in these little settlements got their own supplies over a long, difficult route from Portland. The Northern Pacific Railroad, which was to connect them with all the big cities east and west, was temporarily stalled by financial difficulties. But when the railroad did arrive—and it was expected momentarily through the 1870s—it would be a boon to all these towns.

To one or two of them it would be more than that. It would be another kind of gold mine. It was clear that there would have to be a major distribution point in this inland area, a place where supplies coming in from east and west could be redistributed to all the communities north and south. With its rail links, this town would also likely become a regional manufacturing town and a center for superior law courts, major banks, hospitals, colleges, fine hotels and other urban amenities. Such a town was conspicuous by its absence between the Cascade and Rocky mountain ranges. Many of the new towns of the region fully expected to become metropolises when the railroad arrived.

To do so a town would have to fill two requirements. First, it would have to be within the corridor to be followed by the Northern Pacific line. Then, by growing

Spokane boomed as mining brought increasing white settlement. This is the primitive shaft house of Little Caribou Mine in the 1880s.(EWSHS)

faster than the others, it would have to establish itself as the logical resupply center for all the other towns.

Creating such a town was what James N. Glover and Jasper M. Matheny of Salem, Oregon, had in mind when they set out in the spring of 1873 to scout what was then known as "the wild interior." They rode north on horseback, looking over places where they might establish a new town and new lives. One evening in May the search brought them to the big falls in Spokane country, where a handful of people had set up a little sawmill and established squatter's rights. They were put up in one of the squatter's shacks, and the next morning Glover awoke early to go out and get a view of the falls he had heard thundering all night. He sat and watched the water for two hours, he said later, and when he went back for breakfast, drenched from the spray, he was convinced he had found his place. He and Matheny immediately bought out the squatters and returned to Portland for a bigger sawmill and supplies to open a trading post.

But then, for months on end, not much happened at the little village generally called "the Falls." With no railroad to convey them, new settlers were few and scattered. In 1874, the Reverend Henry T. Cowley opened a school for Indians a short distance from the little store (on what is now Cowley Park). In 1875, the Reverend Samuel Havermale and his wife filed a claim for land that included the island that bears their name. A farmer drifted in here and there to join Moran, Liberty, Lefevre and the other sprinkling of early arrivals. But the new sawmill at the falls could still cut in a week all the lumber the settlers needed in a year. The railroad could save Glover's and Matheny's dream, but after three years there was still no sign of a building crew, and still no proof that the railroad would even come through the Falls.

By 1876 Matheny wanted out. Glover put up everything he had, plus promisory notes, to buy out Matheny and a third partner in Salem. Glover settled in to

Left: *James N. Glover, shown here circa 1878, is known as the father of Spokane. Glover's enthusiasm and ingenuity helped to make Spokane the largest city in the Inland Northwest. In 1881 Glover built his second home on the site of the present Paulsen Medical building. Moved to the corner of First Avenue and Oak Street, Glover's house still stands as the oldest building in the city. (EWSHS)*

continue the vigil by the falls alone. A passer-by of the time remembered this great enterprise, this metropolis of the future, as "a little store with some squaws sitting around the plank platform in front."

By the winter of 1877-1878 Glover still had enough confidence to engage a surveyor to lay out blocks and broad avenues in the fields of tall grass. Basing the whole town on the location of his store, Glover named the street to the north Front because it fronted on the river. (It would later be named Trent and then, just prior to the opening of Expo '74, Spokane Falls Boulevard.) The major north-south street he named for General Oliver O. Howard, the famous Indian fighter who that very winter was pursuing Chief Joseph's rebellious tribe. Glover explained that he had been standing on the platform on that side of the store when he first met General Howard. Glover envisioned the street one block back from the river as the town's center, so he called it Main. Riverside was originally named "South," but was later given the name of its extension to the west, which followed the side of the river. Sprague was named for a general superintendent of the Northern Pacific, a gesture of flattery of the all-powerful railroad officials. Stevens commemorates the territory's first governor. Wall Street was originally called Mill because the sawmill was on the river there. Glover always regretted the change to the more pretentious name.

Post was named for Frederick Post, a German immigrant who moved his flour mill from Post Falls to Spokane Falls (as it was originally called) in 1877. How Post came to Spokane Falls tells something about Glover's determination and why his city survived. A flour mill would lure both sellers of wheat and buyers of flour to a city and was therefore much coveted by all the developing communities. Glover succeeded in persuading Post to move to Spokane Falls by offering the old man no less than a quarter of the whole town. On top of that, Glover donated the lumber for a new mill and helped with the construction.

The following spring, in April of 1878, two men from Portland were in the area scouting opportunities, just as Glover and Matheny had five years earlier. John

Below: *Glover's original 158 acres included most of the present downtown Spokane business district. He purchased the land for $2,000 in 1873, as recorded in this Official Registration of Land Title Patent issued to Glover on April 5, 1878. (EWSHS)*

THE UNITED STATES OF AMERICA,

To all to whom these presents shall come, Greeting:

CERTIFICATE No. 556

Whereas James N. Glover of Stevens County Washington Territory has deposited in the General Land Office of the United States a Certificate of the Register of the Land Office at Walla Walla, Washington Territory whereby it appears that full payment has been made by the said James N. Glover according to the provisions of the Act of Congress of the 24th of April, 1820, entitled "An Act making further provision for the sale of the Public Lands," and the acts supplemental thereto for the South half of the South West quarter, the South West quarter of the South East quarter and the North East quarter of the South West quarter of Section eighteen in Township twenty-five North of Range forty-three East, in the district of lands subject to sale at Walla Walla Washington Territory containing one hundred and fifty-eight acres and thirty-seven hundredths of an acre, according to the Official Plat of the Survey of the said Lands, returned to the General Land Office by the Surveyor General, which said Tract has been purchased by the said James N. Glover.

Now know ye, That the United States of America, in consideration of the premises, and in conformity with the several Acts of Congress in such case made and provided, have given and granted, and by these presents do give and grant unto the said James N. Glover, and to his heirs, the said Tract above described: To have and to hold the same, together with all the rights, privileges, immunities, and appurtenances, of whatsoever nature, thereunto belonging, unto the said James N. Glover and to his heirs and assigns forever; subject to any vested and accrued water rights for mining, agricultural, manufacturing, or other purposes, and rights to ditches and reservoirs used in connection with such water rights, as may be recognized and acknowledged by the local customs, laws, and decisions of courts, and also subject to the right of the proprietor of a vein or lode to extract and remove his ore therefrom, should the same be found to penetrate or intersect the premises hereby granted, as provided by law.

In testimony whereof, I, Rutherford B. Hayes, President of the United States of America, have caused these letters to be made Patent, and the Seal of the General Land Office to be hereunto affixed.

Given under my hand, at the City of Washington, the fifth day of April, in the year of our Lord one thousand eight hundred and seventy-eight, and of the Independence of the United States the one hundred and second.

BY THE PRESIDENT: R. B. Hayes

By B. L. Lang, Secretary.

Recorded, Vol. 1, Page 488.

S. W. Clark, Recorder of the General Land Office.

Right: *Spokane Falls had a total of seven families when Portland, Oregon, attorney J.J. Browne arrived in 1878. Like his partner Anthony M. Cannon, Browne envisioned a potential population of 10,000. He founded the First National Bank, built the first street railway, owned the* Spokane Chronicle, *and joined Cannon to build the Auditorium Theater. He donated the land for Coeur d'Alene Park in the section of Spokane that is his namesake, Browne's Addition. (EWSHS)*

J. Browne and his partner, Anthony Cannon, decided to throw in with Glover. For $3,200 (mostly on credit) they bought half of Glover's remaining townsite. Browne also filed a homestead claim for land at the west edge of Glover's land—"Browne's Addition"—and Cannon put in a claim for land on the hill at the south edge of town.

Browne, an attorney who had served a term as superintendent of schools in Portland, was levelheaded and ambitious. Cannon was not so levelheaded but made up for it by being twice as ambitious. He was full of ideas, good ones and bad ones, and history has been unkind to him merely because he had an inclination toward the latter. Shortly after he arrived he mistook wildflowers swaying in a night breeze for feathers on Indians' heads and got the whole village into an uproar with warnings of an attack. It was probably the last time he was ever overly cautious. He opened the first bank in Spokane Falls soon after arriving, but being considerably underfinanced, it was also the first bank to go broke.

Cannon would have to be counted as the main irritant as well as the main booster of the little town—if it hadn't been for the arrival of a feisty twenty-eight-year-old editor by the name of Francis Cook. Little wonder that the two men were soon drawing swords. Cook printed something (what it was we don't know) that Cannon took exception to—violent exception, as they say, because Cannon and his son-in-law went to Cook's offices with a loaded gun. Cook persuaded them to leave by belting them with a press iron and kicking them down the stairway.

An editor, even a bad tempered one, was an impressive recruitment to the city. Cook had come through on a general inspection tour in 1879 and was charmed by the place; Glover hooked him by donating both lots on the east side of Howard between Riverside and Sprague for newspaper offices.

By now others were choosing to settle here without such inducements. Dr. Joseph Gandy, a physician from Tacoma seeking a drier climate, built an office on Howard (with a second story for his family to live in) and gave Spokane a doctor's services. Seattle's city attorney, Colonel David P. Jenkins, defected to Spokane in 1880. Jenkins, a dapper, cane-carrying Civil War hero, was the

Left: *An ambitious pioneer and businessman, Anthony M. Cannon built the huge Auditorium Theater, founded the Spokane & Palouse Railroad, started the Bank of Spokane Falls, and presided as mayor of the city. (EWSHS)*

Far left: *This sawmill on the river near present-day Post Street Bridge, where James Glover turned out timber for the first buildings in 1874, is the site of the founding of the town of Spokane. By 1884, when this lithograph was drawn, Anthony M. Cannon was proprietor. (EWSHS)*

first to stake a claim on the north side of the river, a claim that included all the land around the present courthouse. The same year, W.C. Gray, a hotelier in Redding, California, came through to look and promptly bought the choice lot on the northeast corner of Front and Howard.

By 1880 "the Falls"—as most early residents called it—had a population of 350. Its streets were busier than that number would seem to warrant because homesteaders, prospectors, and other visitors come through daily. It was the dusty little Western town that forms the backdrop of hundreds of movies and novels of the Old West. A visitor that summer, if he had no personal conveyance, would arrive by stage. After an all-day journey up from Colfax in a cramped, swaying little car, he would jump down in front of the new stage and telegraph offices on the south side of Front Street. These buildings, like most of the buildings in town, were made of newly cut and unpainted pine. If the traveler asked the stage driver—wiry little Louis Yake, who carried both a bowie knife and a pistol in his belt—where there was a hotel, Louis would point to the corner across the street. The two-story building there had a fresh coat of paint and was made the more inviting by a wide, shaded porch that ran all along the front and wrapped around the side. The hotel butted up against the river, and behind it, where Howard came to the river, the visitor would see a messy little backwater where logs and bark float together in the still water.

The California Hotel stood on the corner now occupied by the Carousel. Looking south from that corner, up Howard, one would see most of the town—three blocks of solidly packed wooden buildings. Signs on the big squared-off false fronts and on windows read "Jack Squire's Saloon," "McCammon and Whitman Men's Clothing," "R.W. Rima, Jeweler," "Graham's—Grocery, Liquors, Tobaccos."

In the whole town there were about fifty buildings, barely enough to keep the emptiness of the surrounding country at bay. Most of them were one story and cast little shade on the wide streets. The whole place baked under a hot sun.

The talk that summer and fall of 1880 was of two things: the arrival of the railroad from the west, which finally seemed imminent, and the elections. Jimmy Glover and some other boosters had gone to Olympia and persuaded the legislature to create a new county out of a number of unwieldy counties that already existed. Spokane Falls had begun to take a leadership role in the region; its designation as county seat, to be formalized in an election that fall, would be its formal investiture.

But then there was trouble. About seventeen miles to the southwest, on the anticipated route of the Northern Pacific Railroad, there appeared some stacks of lumber, and then some frame buildings, and then a town, more or less. The new settlement announced it would call itself Cheney, after a Northern Pacific official. It also let it be known it would like to become the county seat. No one considered Cheney a serious contender in the county seat ballot until the town recruited to its cause a formidable editor in Colfax by the name of Lucien E. Kellogg. Kellogg hitched his presses to horses, like field artillery, and set out for Cheney. Having no building there, he set the presses up under a tree and began to bombard Spokane Falls. Kellogg reported that a Falls man had been overheard saying flatly his town didn't want the business of farmers. "Farmers, [the story concluded] will you vote for Spokane Falls when it has told you it doesn't want your support?"

Spokane Times editor Francis Cook unlimbered his own guns and began to return in kind. "Cheney is a spot in the wilderness where an imaginary town exists," he reported to his readers after a visit there. Back and forth it went, in the two papers, along the roads, in bars, in farm-by-farm visits by emissaries of the two towns, until November 2, 1880, election day. The vote: Spokane Falls 563, Cheney, 680.

Spokane Falls was stunned. The bright future it had mapped out for itself seemed in danger. But the gloom was brief. The votes had to be certified by the auditor, and the auditor, a Falls man by the name of James M. Nosler, found that there were certain problems with votes from some of the precincts. He disqualified the votes of those precincts, and the result was to reverse the outcome of the election. Spokane Falls sent word to Cheney that it had lost after all.

Cheney swore all kinds of reprisals, but in the end only brought a lawsuit. The judgment was in Cheney's favor, and Spokane Falls was ordered to turn over

This 1884 view looks north from Howard Street and Front Avenue (now Spokane Falls Boulevard) toward Havermale Island. Spokane's first hotel, the California Hotel, stood to the east of the bridge. The Echo Roller Mills, built in 1883 and later owned by Albert Keats, utilized the river's power to grind flour, and was considered Spokane's most prominent building at that time. (EWSHS)

Francis H. Cook, Spokane's first editor, was naturally combative and seems to have riled nearly everyone in town at one time or another. Anthony Cannon once appeared at Cook's newspaper office with pistol in hand to demand a retraction of something Cook had said in the Spokane Times. *Cook declined to make the retraction, and then knocked Cannon back down the stairs with a press iron. (EWSHS)*

the county records forthwith.

History long ago decided, quite reasonably, that Spokane Falls had tried to steal the election (or at least steal it back, since Falls citizens believed that Cheney won only because railroad workers were transferred in by the Northern Pacific for the purpose of helping its chosen town on election day). Nosler himself maintained that he only ruled as the law said he must rule and didn't even know the outcome of the final vote until after his decision had been made.

The week of Cheney's victory in court there was a heavy snowfall that covered Spokane Falls to a depth of ten inches. James Nosler loaded his wife and two children aboard a large sled and they rode from their house east of town to spend an evening at Jimmy Glover's house.

Glover's little house stood next to the stagecoach office at Front and Howard. We can imagine the no-doubt distracted auditor being greeted at the door by the perennially jovial Glover. If we could just follow them into the parlor and listen to their conversation that night, it is intriguing to think, we might learn more about these men and their motives in the election in one hour than we know after a hundred years. But history leaves us standing outside.

The most we ever get to tell us what these historic characters were really like is a kind of glance through the window—some little insight, perhaps from a letter or diary, that gives us a look at a real human being. It may be fragmentary but it is vivid—and it tells us things we never learned from documents and official statements. The letters of John J. Browne to his wife, for example, are filled with passages like: "This day perhaps has filled many a soul with joy and happiness, but I am lonely—my every thought is of you and darling little Guy. I hope you have kissed him, for me, many times today." After reading such passages the view one gets is unmistakably of the gentle-faced man with thinning hair hoisting and playing with his son.

There is no such clear view of Glover—the private man, that is, as opposed to the ebullient founder his contemporaries always describe. Through all the histories his family life remains a mystery. His wife is mentioned as being in Spokane with him in the early years, but soon she fades from the histories entirely. Recently a researcher in Oregon found that Susan Glover suffered "periods of despondency" as a young woman and spent the last years of her life in Oregon under supervision, mentally ill. Glover supported her with checks sent from Spokane. The picture of Glover is still not clear, but there is a humanizing sadness in this researcher's discovery that does not come through in other versions of Spokane history.

We have a better view of the other man in the room that snowy night, auditor James Nosler. He began to keep a diary when he entered the Union Army in

Glover Block, one of the first brick buildings in Spokane, was built by James Glover in 1883. The building stood on the southwest corner of Howard Street and Front Avenue (now Spokane Falls Boulevard), directly across Howard Street from Glover's original trading post. (EWSHS)

1860 and it became a lifelong habit. The story it traces is twice valuable, both as the story of a single person, and as a story that is as typical of all pioneers as any individual's story is likely to be.

He emerged from the war determined to marry the girl he loved, though her parents were against it, and find his place in the world. He tried operating a general store in Iowa but soon concluded, as he said in his diary, "I can never stand this kind of do-nothing life." So he decided to try his luck out West. In 1870 he bought tickets on the just-completed Union Pacific Railroad to California and took his wife and three-year-old daughter, Flora, to the fabled West. That first night on the train, as he rolled toward the West, he wrote in his diary: "We are going to Oregon—not to find a Paradise, but a home among its mountains where Sallie can have better health and we can lay up something for the future, for the education of our children, and our own comfort should we live to become old."

He took his family from California to Oregon and then finally to Washington Territory, engaging in a number of occupations ranging from teaching school to

lumbering and farming. But the dream didn't work as it was supposed to. Often his children went hungry. Settled in Colfax in 1877, he wrote in his diary, "It seems as though I can never make another raise. I have tried almost everything, but the mines. Verily the first thousand is harder to get than the next ten thousand."

That winter, in a passage that ran several pages of his diary, he described the death of the daughter he had brought West with him:

At 9 p.m. Dr. came over. After examining her he called Sallie out and told her that our little lamb would not live through the day. Her legs and hands and face were getting cold then . . . She asked for her hoarhound candy and took a bite off of it. She then raised up by my assistance and looked at her Ma, who asked her if she saw her. She said yes. Her ma then asked her if she 'wanted to go and be with Aunt Ella.' She faintly whispered 'yes.' I asked her if she wanted to go and live with the angels. Again she whispered 'yes!' And just then I think the veil between her and heaven was removed. She looked upward with a look of wonderment and awe on her face and passed away without a struggle, only a few long breaths . . . She died on my left arm and her ma holding her by the hand. Her last movement was to put her right hand to her head as though it itched . . . .

Below, left: *The clearing and grading crew for the first Northern Pacific Railroad through Spokane met this basalt outcropping just east of the present Amtrak depot at First Avenue and Bernard Street in 1881. It was one of the many obstacles the teams had to overcome in the Spokane area. The first train from the east came through the city in the summer of 1883. (EWSHS)*

The next year, in October of 1878, Nosler moved his family to Spokane Falls, becoming one of its earliest settlers. He homesteaded the property east of Division and south of the river, opened a land agent office, and built an office next to the California Hotel. He was in poor health. ("This morning I coughed up blood—the first time since that time in Oregon," he wrote in his diary February 17, 1879. "When there is anything the matter with me my great concern is for my family. I want to live as much to provide for them and get them in comfortable circumstances and beyond reach of want, as much as anything else.") Yet he became involved in a half a dozen enterprises in Spokane Falls, ranging from his real estate business to jobbing wood and contracting to build buildings. This was the man Spokane Falls appointed county auditor, and who ever since has been known to history only as "J.M. Nosler," the man who cheated Cheney in the county seat election.

Nosler's place in history was guaranteed a few months later. Spokane Falls citizens were moving slowly on the certification—perhaps hoping to hang on until it could be reasonably argued that a second vote should be held—so Cheney citizens, who lacked numbers but never nerve, took direct action. One night in March when nearly everybody in Spokane Falls was at a wedding party a group of Cheney volunteers walked quietly up Main Street. After a quick recount of the votes, with the aid of Nosler's successor, (Nosler had resigned), the Cheney men peremptorily declared Cheney the winner of the election, stacked the records on wagons, and took them home with them. The records, and thus the official county seat, remained in Cheney until the second election was held in 1886.

Spokane residents felt that the town's growth had been arrested by the loss of the county seat because many settlers

Above: *This 1888 view of Spokane was taken at Pioneer Park, above Seventh Avenue looking north on Howard Street. The white two-story building two blocks down on the right is the Spokane School House, on the present site of Lewis & Clark High School. (EWSHS)*

Right: *When the city of Spokane decided to fund a college in 1881, Father Joseph Cataldo grew concerned about the strong Protestant influence in the area. Gonzaga was finally established by the Jesuits in 1887, and shown here in April of 1890. (EWSHS)*

Left: *The Comet Hose Team, also known as the Tigers, was Spokane Falls' first volunteer fire department, organized in the 1880s. This picture was taken on Mill Street (now Wall), along the east side of A.M. Cannon's Bank of Spokane Falls. A boy and dalmatian ride along as mascots for the team. (EWSHS)*

and businessmen chose to settle in Cheney. But that year of 1881 was nevertheless a signal one in Spokane's history. The city got its first brick building, the Wolverton on the corner of Riverside and Mill (Wall), and its first bridge, an island-hopping affair that started at the foot of Howard Street. And late that year the city of Spokane Falls was officially incorporated by the state legislature.

Most important of all, it was in the spring of 1881 that the Northern Pacific Railroad tracks were at long last completed through Spokane. Glover's little town was at last linked to the wider world. This link would be completed two years later when the western and eastern branches of the Northern Pacific met in Montana. After 1883 anyone in any Eastern city could be in Spokane in a matter of days, and in reasonable comfort. This spurred a tremendous boost in population. In 1888 alone over 1,000 people filed homestead claims for government-owned land in the Spokane Falls office.

Some people had warned Glover that the falls, though beautiful, might be a disadvantage to a city if the railroads considered them an obstacle. Luckily, Glover paid no attention, and just a few years later these falls turned out to be an asset that no one could have anticipated. Even as Glover was founding his little city, Thomas Edison and others were perfecting the mechanisms for providing commercial electricity. When the technology was ready in the early 1880s, Spokane Falls found that it had a power source right in its midst. The town had electric street lights by 1886, making it one of the first electrified cities in the West.

The spring and summer of 1885 saw the discovery of the first two "hard rock" mines in the area—the Old Dominion a few miles from Colville and the fabulous Bunker Hill in the Coeur d'Alene Mountains. A stampede of gold-seekers fol-

Above: *Spokane Falls experienced a period of accelerated growth in 1887. This photo was taken from the top of Echo Mill, looking east and south. Havermale Island sits in the left foreground. The two-story structure on the near horizon is the first Sacred Heart Hospital. (EWSHS)*

Right: *Possibly the only photograph existing of the great Spokane fire of August 4, 1889, this view looks north on Howard Street from Railroad Avenue, about one block east of where the fire started. The street was cluttered with furniture and goods that had been cleared from the buildings that stood in the fire's path. (EWSHS)*

Right: *Workmen prepare to open the vault of James Glover's First National Bank, on the corner of Howard Street and Riverside Avenue. The vault was not opened until several days after the fire because of retained heat within the safe. Notice the armed guard standing in the ruins at left. (EWSHS)*

lowed, and mining would join agriculture in making Spokane Falls rich.

It was not, however, preordained that the wealth from the area's ore and grain be channeled through Spokane. While Spokane lay right between the great farmland and mining districts, it was by the same token close to neither. That disadvantage was neutralized by aggressive railroad building that soon made Spokane Falls the most convenient shipping point for thousands of farmers and tens of thousands of miners. Glover and several partners reached north with a railroad to the Okanogan mines. Cannon helped organize a railroad serving the farm towns of the Palouse. The newcomer Daniel C. Corbin pushed Spokane's influence eastward by building rails to the Coeur d'Alene mining district.

Now most of the business of this booming region would be channeled through Spokane. Between 1886 and 1889 the population of Spokane went from 3,500 to 20,000. Shacks, apartments, hotels and rooming houses sprung up in every vacant spot. Shops and offices expanded and proliferated to employ the newcomers. In 1889 Spokane Falls had six banks, twelve blacksmiths, fifteen barbers, four cigar factories, thirty groceries, ten lunch counters, sixteen restaurants and three theaters. The most widespread businesses were real estate offices (thirty) and saloons (forty).

Those quiet streets of 1880 now churned with life: cable and horse-drawn tramways plowed their way through the traffic; farmers loaded buckboards; sidewalks were crowded with miners, drifters, businessmen, Chinese, Indians (the famed Chief Joseph, assigned to the Colville Reservation after his defeat, was seen on these streets), messenger boys, prostitutes, shopkeepers, shoppers, and a constant parade of immigrants, satchels in hand.

A Sunday morning, particularly a hot, languorous one like August 4, 1889, would have been one of the few times things were quiet. Even the little flame that started up in a restaurant by the railroad depot seemed lazy. A man who saw it right after it started said a stream from a garden hose would have put it out easily.

But there was no stream forthcoming. The water that fed all the city's new fire hydrants (a matter of considerable pride) had been shut off, and the only man who seemed to know how to turn it on was out of town.

The flame grew, leapt across the street, took hold in a row of wooden buildings, then spread through the whole block. Some buildings were dynamited in an effort to cut the blaze off. When that had little effect, it became apparent that nothing was going to stop the blaze. The population, all except the two who died in the flames, escaped across the river or out into the fields. As night fell the fire was crested over the roofs of the city and shot burning timbers into the air like rockets. Only some quick dousings saved the buildings on the north side of the river.

The next day Spokane Falls was a twelve-square-block cinder. Some people hiked up the rail line and left by train forever. Slowly those who stayed moved in to explore: they found ragged brick walls and still-steaming telephone poles standing like ghosts in drifting smoke; a pile of black timber and metals at the middle of each lot; and little else except the acrid smell of roasted wood. James N. Glover had gone from youth to middle age building the city. Friday he and the other city builders had left desks piled high with plans and prospects. Now, Monday, they had no plans, no prospects—no desks! Everything that had occupied their minds for a decade had come to a halt as sudden and strange as death itself.

III

• Fortunes •

Facing page: *Jacob "Dutch Jake" Goetz (standing on bottom step near banister) and his partner Harry Baer (to Goetz's left) posed with employees and customers in the lobby of their Coeur d'Alene Theater in 1894. As saloon owners in northern Idaho, Goetz and Baer provided a down-and-out Noah Kellogg with a small grubstake, in exchange for a portion of the prospector's findings. Jake's settlement from Kellogg's Bunker Hill strike alone ended up at nearly $200,000. The partners brought their money to Spokane, investing in this gambling hall at Trent Avenue and Howard Street. The establishment reportedly challenged "any fun place north of Denver," and included a variety theater, Turkish baths, dance hall, and food and liquor counters. (EWSHS)*

The gloom and shock of the fire were short-lived. Immediately those who had built the city took the lead in rebuilding it, and in the first year following the fire approximately 100 brick buildings were under construction in downtown Spokane. The city that was built over the next couple of years—buildings with red brick facades, studded with granite blocks and dignified by arched windows in upper stories—was the city Spokanites would know for the next eighty years, until the Expo '74 renewal. Traces of the old city are still there: in the "1889 Building" at the corner of Main and Stevens, the Bennett Block (1890) at Main and Howard, the Kuhn Building (1890), and the Review Building (1891).

In 1891, the city council shortened the city's name by dropping the "Falls." To draw the rapidly developing North Side into the city, the council ordered up no fewer than five new bridges that year, including a spindly Monroe Street Bridge on iron stilts.

Everyone was in an expansive mood. While the city constructed a new city hall (later to be razed for the railroad station on Front Avenue), white bricks from Clayton kilns were forming a fine French renaissance structure to house county government and courts. The cost of $376,000 was twice what the new city hall cost, and it raised some eyebrows. But it was a bargain, being that rare example of truly distinguished small-town civic architecture.

The boom of the mid-1880s had given the founders of the city some working capital and unlimited confidence that it would all happen again. Jimmy Glover took to wearing a top hat and built a mansion, Spokane's first, a rambling Tudor estate on the unsettled slope south of town. Anthony Cannon, of course, outdid that. He and John J. Browne ushered in Spokane's "Age of Elegance," as it has been called, by building the Auditorium, a cavernous theater draped in velvet and gold gilt.

The founders were able to rebuild in such style because among the farmers who had done well in the Palouse were some Dutch immigrants. These Dutchmen wrote home with praise for the potential of the land, but complained about 10 percent interest rates. Hearing about those rates and the demand, Dutch bankers sent representatives on the next boat with orders to loan whatever they could.

With the silver mines, agriculture, and trade all booming, investing in Spokane should have been the safe bet the Dutch thought it was. Then came what was known as the Panic of 1893. Around the world enthusiasm for buying and selling suddenly cooled. New York stock values collapsed and in nearly every town and village in the country people withdrew their money from banks to put it in a safe place.

Cannon's Marble Bank, having used a larger share of depositor's cash on ventures than any other in town, very quickly went under. News of this sent anyone in town who might have considered keeping a cool head running to the wire cages of all the other banks in town. Glover's First National Bank held on manfully for a few days and finally had to give up.

Right: *These brickmakers are from the J.T. Davie & Company brickyard, in 1890. The brickyard, located about three miles west of Spokane on Medical Lake Road, provided the brick for most of Spokane's buildings in the 1880s and 1890s. (EWSHS)*

Right, below: *Appropriately named, the Granite Block was constructed from granite brought in from within a fifty-mile radius of Spokane. The building stood on the southwest corner of Washington Street and Riverside Avenue, the original site of James Glover's 1881 home. (EWSHS)*

Facing page, top: *The Empire State Building, now known as the Great Western Building, seen in the background, was built in 1900 on the original site of the Commercial Hotel, and claimed to have the fastest elevators west of Chicago at that time. Notice that in this 1901 view of Riverside Avenue and Monroe Street, the south end of the Monroe Street Bridge, on the far left in this picture, extends nearly to Riverside Avenue. (EWSHS)*

Meanwhile, the Dutch bankers, themselves a little panicked, demanded immediate repayment of all loans. Since their cash had already been taken by depositors, one after another the Spokane bankers turned over their assets. Eventually a quarter of the city, incuding many of the major buildings on Riverside, was owned by a clutch of Dutch bankers on the other side of the world. To make the ill-fortune complete, a series of bad seasons in the 1890s bankrupted many of the early farmers of the area.

For the second time in four years the original city builders were wiped out. Some of them, the purposeful John J. Browne and the shrewd James Monaghan, for example, eventually recovered their fortunes. Glover became a civic elder, honored with directorships and a stint on the city council, but was never truly part of the city's top leadership again. He had lived in his mansion just months before he had to give it up to pay the bank's debts. Cannon left Spokane and traveled as far as South America looking for another stake so that he could begin again. In April of 1895 people back home got the word that he died alone and poor in a New York City hotel room.

That year also saw the death of Frank R. Moore, one of the original storekeepers at Howard and Front along with Cannon and Glover. Like Cannon and Glover, Moore went into banking and like them he was ruined in the panic. He died of a painful stomach problem, at the age of forty-three, leaving his widow with a tangled mass of debts.

What was lost by some generally came into the possession of others, creating wholesale turnover in Spokane's leadership. The court-appointed receiver for

The Spokane County Courthouse Building, on Broadway between Jefferson and Madison streets, was constructed in 1894. The huge maple trees currently surrounding the courthouse are mere sprigs in this 1899 photograph. (EWSHS)

Frank Moore's affairs was F. Lewis Clark. Clark would handle the complex affairs masterfully, save the Last Chance Mine for the Moore estate, and in the process make himself a millionaire.

Clark was forerunner of a new leadership in Spokane. Harvard educated and financed by his banker father, he had come West in 1885, at the age of twenty-six, and opened a flour mill (the C and C Mill on Havermale Island) even as he strategically bought up real estate in the frontier city.

Daniel C. Corbin and the first William H. Cowles were of the same stripe. Corbin, whose mansion in Pioneer Park now belongs to the city, was older than most of the new wave of leaders, being fifty-seven when he arrived in Spokane in 1888. The face we see in photographs of him—trim beard around a firm mouth; strands of white hair laying across the pate like drifting smoke; unblinking eyes that stare back and seem to say "state your business and move on"—is a fair reflection of a flinty personality. If this was the "Inland Empire," here was the face of an emperor. Corbin was from an established New York family; a brother had built the railroad to Coney Island. But there was no family fortune, so Corbin had spent his whole life in the various enterprises required to develop a frontier.

In Spokane he pushed railroads out into the mining districts to tap for the city the wealth flowing from them. Then at the age of sixty-seven he became intrigued with the idea of making Spokane's agriculture bloom. He tried to establish the sugar beet industry here. It proved a costly flop, but led Corbin and a partner into pioneering one of the great success stories of the time: the irrigation of the Spokane Valley. He was thought a little zany for even trying, but by 1900 the first ditch was carrying water from Liberty Lake the six and a half miles to a farm dubbed "Green Acres."

Cowles had in common with Corbin his almost accidental appearance in Spokane. The *Review,* established in 1883 by a good newspaperman by the name of Frank Dallam, ended up in the hands of Harvey Scott, the opinionated and powerful publisher of Portland's *Oregonian.* That Spokane's major newspaper should be in the hands of a publisher from an enemy city—Portland was a competitor for dominance of the market to Spokane's southwest—was considered intolerable by many Spokanites. A group of them lured two *Chicago Tribune* journalists to Spokane to start another newspaper. They in turn, finding themselves with financial problems soon after starting the *Spokesman,* called in another partner—the first William Hutchinson Cowles. Aside from family money, Cowles brought to the enterprise the unusual combination of a Yale law degree and experience as a police reporter on the *Tribune.*

Meanwhile, Scott began to build a new headquarters, a red brick edifice with a higher steeple than that of the church it replaced at that corner. The cost of the new building, the *Spokesman's* challenge, and the economic slump of the early 1890s soon had the *Review* under financial pressure. It was reportedly Scott's editor, N.W. Durham, who first approached Cowles and his partners about a merger to stop the murderous competition. The papers were combined, and soon thereafter everyone but Cowles seemed to lose their enthusiasm for Spokane journalism. Cowles bought them out. Five years later he purchased the *Chronicle* from John J. Browne and his partners and became the city's only publisher.

Much later, after World War I, Cowles would help maintain for Spokane its reputation as an extremely conservative community. But as a young publisher he was well out in front of the community's leadership on many issues. Under his leadership *The Spokesman-Review* urged liberal public expenditure on education, parks and public libraries, advocated a "windfall tax" on excessive earnings from land speculation, and endorsed the radical populist William Jennings Bryan for the presidency in 1896.

Of course, that endorsement of Bryan at least partly reflected the fact that Bryan's idea of allowing the unlimited coining of silver wasn't radical in Spokane. The city was quickly becoming the silver capital of the United States. The strikes of gold, silver and lead made in the 1880s were now, in the mid-1890s, being turned into huge mining operations with the help of Eastern seaboard capital. By 1896, the Bunker Hill, Sullivan, and a half dozen other mines in the Coeur d'Alene were producing 11,000 tons of silver-lead concentrates a month. That same year, the giant War Eagle and Le Roi mines just over the Canadian border in Rossland paid their first dividends to Spokane owners. Between 1895 and 1920, the mines of the area would produce well over one billion dollars in turn-of-the-

Left: *After he came to Spokane Falls in 1888, D.C. (Daniel Chase) Corbin started building railroads to the north and east. These railroads made possible the development of mines that later produced millions of dollars, much of which came to Spokane. Corbin's estate was estimated at over $12 million at the time of his death in 1918, and included the Cutter-built mansion overlooking the city above Seventh Avenue. (EWSHS)*

Facing page, top: *Building the Auditorium Theater was Anthony M. Cannon's most impressive achievement. Construction of the theater began in 1889 and was nearly completed before the great fire ruined what had been built. The reconstructed Auditorium was finally opened in 1892, and in the following decade it boasted the largest stage of any theater west of the Mississippi. (EWSHS)*

Facing page, bottom: *The opulent interior of the Auditorium Theater signaled Spokane's dawning "Age of Elegance." (EWSHS)*

Right: *Irish-born pioneer James Monaghan, seated at right, posed with his family for this portrait in the 1890s. Monaghan immigrated to the U.S. in 1856, and his shrewd investments made him rich. (EWSHS)*

Below: *Construction began in 1892 on what was to be the new home of A.M. Cannon's Bank of Spokane Falls. Unfortunately, Cannon never got the chance to move his bank into the new building, since his was the first to close its doors in the Panic of 1893. During the next sixty years the Marble Bank did house a number of financial institutions. (EWSHS)*

century dollars, and a good portion of it would stay in Spokane.

Spokane was to the mines what a theater headquarters is to the battlefield. Far removed from the blasting and daily assaults against the mountains, it was, nevertheless, where the generals gathered to lay their strategies. There were some 200 mining offices in the city at the turn of the century.

This is also where the miners came to escape the bleakness of the dusty mining camps. They congregated along the riverfront, where pool halls and hock shops were separated by dark and steamy saloons. Front Avenue alone had five large houses of ill repute. A little to the east, the area bounded by Howard, Bernard,

Front and Main, was called "Oriental Alley." Here, scattered liberally among laundries and other businesses operated by Chinese (who had been recruited to build the railroads, then cast aside), were opium dens and more houses of prostitution.

The best of the many gambling houses was Dutch Jake's, which by the mid-1890s was in its permanent home in the Coeur d'Alene Hotel (the building, now taller, still stands at the southeast corner of Howard and Spokane Falls Boulevard). It was four stories of big mirrors, long bars, good booze, green gambling tables, and glittering chandeliers. Cards were dealt by pretty women who wore tuxedo coats but no shirts, a costume that became a public issue, though the move to disallow it never succeeded. Jake himself was a good citizen and decent man who never turned away a cold or hungry human being.

Dutch Jake's was a public palace where miners in from poorly-lit and cold shacks could live like royalty for a few hours. Their employers, the owners of the mines, also came to Spokane to pursue their fantasies. But they had no need for Dutch Jake's. Million-dollar gambles—buying and selling mines—were part of their daily business. And they could afford their own palaces, sumptuous mansions designed for them by a slightly built, quiet aesthete named Kirtland Cutter.

Cutter had intended to become an artist, an ambition which saved him from Yale, where his grandfather was a distinguished alumnus. Instead he briefly studied art in New York and London and then drifted through Europe making sketches of the landscape and buildings. A few years later he returned to the U.S. and traveled again, this time west. He arrived in Spokane in 1885, where an uncle was an officer in Jimmy Glover's bank. He brought with him a trunk full of fancy clothes and (for he was prematurely bald) a set of exchangeable toupees graduated in length to suggest growth. He worked briefly as a bank clerk and then went to work for an architect. Though he had no formal training in architecture, Jimmy Glover hired him to design his mansion. Cutter created a homey castle on the South Hill which established his

Left: *Pioneer miner Patrick "Patsy" Clark was born in Ireland on St. Patrick's Day in 1850. Clark ventured into the southwestern United States, where he started and operated several gold and copper mines. He migrated northward in the 1880s, working mines in Montana, British Columbia, northern Idaho, and Washington. (EWSHS)*

Below: *In 1890, the* Review *newspaper office was housed in this small wooden structure, on the southeast corner of Riverside Avenue and Monroe Street. The steepled First Presbyterian Church was torn down later that year, and replaced by the Review Tower in 1891. (EWSHS)*

John Finch, along with his partner Amasa B. Campbell, acquired a considerable fortune from his mines in northern Idaho. Finch used some of the money to have Kirtland Cutter build him a white-pillared home at the west end of First Avenue. Finch's estate at the time of his death totaled well over $3 million, 40 percent of which he left to charity and various civic enterprises. Upon the closing of the Finch estate, $250,000 was given to the city park board to develop the Finch Memorial Arboretum, south of the Sunset Highway. (EWSHS)

reputation as Spokane's mansion builder.

Henry C. Bertelson, head draftsman for Cutter for fifteen years, said of his boss: "He never did any mechanical drawing nor did he ever use a square or a triangle. He carried a short, stubby pencil around in his shirt pocket [while on a building site] and when he had an idea he made his sketches."

In this way Cutter created, from his memories of European architecture, the buildings Spokane values most to this day. These include, to name a few examples, both Corbin homes and the F. Lewis Clark house on Seventh Avenue; the Graves and Davenport mansions on the north side of town (the latter is now part of St. George's school); and many of the most distinctive buildings downtown, including the Sherwood Building, the Catholic Diocesan headquarters, the Chronicle Building, and (his masterpiece) the Davenport Hotel. In each there is the beauty of conception and attention to detail that are the marks of art.

Cutter's designs provided Spokane's growing *nouveau riche* with instant heritage. Patsy Clark, for example, the tough Irish immigrant who battled miners to a draw as manager of mines from Butte to Burke, and whose great renown stemmed from his stealing for Simeon Reed of Portland an advance sample of the Bunker Hill mine, could survey his own success as he stepped into the house Cutter fashioned for him on Coeur d'Alene Park. Cutter had made a trip around the world to pick out the materials and furnishings: bricks from St. Louis, the stained glass window and fixtures from Tiffany's of New York, the grandfather clock and other furniture from London, rugs from Turkey, and stonework from Italy. To paint the ceiling in the Louis XIV room he brought a muralist from France.

At the threshold of these mansions the dust and mud of the West gave way to new refinements. Wives who, like Mrs. Clark, had spent their first married years in rough mining camps, now planned elaborate formal parties and went calling on each other in their fancy buggies—a social custom for which a gaudy room just inside the front entrance was set aside. Evenings they would strap themselves into a body vise known as a whalebone corset for a performance at the Auditorium, thence to Davenport's Restaurant, where trout in big aquariums swam back and forth staring at diners.

A few blocks away from Patsy Clark's house Cutter was building, also in 1898, mansions for the biggest Northwest mining operators of all, the partners Finch and Campbell. For John Finch, Cutter designed a plantation-style mansion at the end of First Avenue, with imposing white columns and lawns spreading in every direction. For Amasa B. Campbell, Cutter created the solemn Tudor enclave that is now the county museum's best exhibit.

Visitors who inspect this mansion—its luminous Louis XIV sitting room, its ducal living room, its displays of fine China

Left: *Mine owner Amasa B. Campbell posed with his five-year-old daughter, Helen, in 1897. With John Finch, Campbell had extensive holdings in the Coeur d'Alene mountains, including the Hecla, Gem, and Kendall mines. Since 1925 Campbell's home, designed by Kirtland Cutter, has been known as the Grace Campbell Memorial Museum. (EWSHS)*

and the silk dresses—imagine an "Age of Elegance," as the era has been called. But much as the man who inhabited this model of an English gentleman's house might enjoy the role, Campbell was not a country gentleman. The mines attracted the ambitious, the smart, and the greedy from every corner of the country. Some innocents had stumbled into fortunes. But most could not depend upon luck. Campbell had lived in mining camps from Mexico to Alaska and was forty-five before he underwent the softening influences of wealth and marriage. He had lured his partner Finch and a handful of rich Ohio investors to the Coeur d'Alenes with promises of big returns, promises he was expected to keep.

Below: *This view looks north on Howard Street, between Sprague and First avenues, in the 1890s. The Symons Building appears prominently on the right. (EWSHS)*

Right: *On April 19, 1899, hundreds of disgruntled mine workers took control of the Bunker Hill Mine, at Wardner, Idaho, and planted explosives throughout the facility. (EWSHS)*

Right: *Colonel William H. Ridpath used his profits from the Le Roi Gold Mine to build an elegant hotel on First Avenue in 1899 between Howard and Stevens streets. The original Ridpath Hotel burned in 1950, but was rebuilt immediately on the same site. (EWSHS)*

Facing page, bottom: *This photograph of early Spokane mayors was taken in 1910. Pictured are: (Back row, left to right) Charles Fleming, Charles Fassett, C. Herbert Moore, W.J. Hindley, and (front row, left to right) David B. Fotheringham, James N. Glover, Daniel Drumheller, and Charles Clough. (EWSHS)*

In 1899, the year after the mansion was completed, Campbell was fighting refinery trusts trying to keep his ore out of the market on one hand, while he was dealing with miners constantly on the verge of rebellion on the other.

The rebellion came on April 29, 1899. When the manager of the Bunker Hill Mine refused to give recognition to a union, a well-organized group of masked men hijacked a Northern Pacific train which was headed for the Bunker Hill. They used it to carry hundreds of armed men and dozens of boxes of dynamite to the mine. The men seized the mine with little trouble and stacked the dynamite inside the huge processing buildings at its mouth. Someone pushed a plunger and the buildings were reduced to slivers.

Campbell rushed to the Coeur d'Alene to organize the defense of his own mines. He was armed and personally led a horseback chase of some of the outlaw miners. Only when he was sure things were under control in the mountains did he return to Spokane to organize a counterattack.

He figured the mines would be closed for a time. "I do not care," he wrote one of his partners, "this fight had to come."

Campbell and the other mine owners met and agreed to lock all strikers and sympathizers out and recruit all new employees. Campbell's partner, John Finch, was dispatched to San Francisco to begin recruiting workers. Meanwhile, at the goading of powerful mine owners, federal and state officials declared martial law in the mining district and rounded up hundreds of miners—mostly without proof that they had been a part of the assault on the Bunker Hill. The miners were kept in a makeshift prison at Wardner indiscriminantly and indefinitely—violation enough of basic rights even in those rough-and-tumble circumstances to prompt a Congressional investigation a year later.

The kind of power these mining lords could wield is suggested in a letter Campbell wrote to a partner in July:

... The Governor was up to Wallace with me and I read him your letter in regard to seeing the President. .. He informs me that he has already commenced corresponding with the administration to keep the soldiers there all next year at least, and he intends to continue martial law during his term of office. He intends that every man who ever belonged to the Miners' Union, and who was connected with these outrages, shall leave the country. The old sheriff and county commissioners have all been removed and we have a new set of county officials. The present board of county commissioners will see that no man gets a license to run a saloon in the country unless he can give excellent bonds and even in that case there will be very few saloons started. These places have always been the headquarters for plotting and nearly every saloon man in the country is an anarchist.

The deadly seriousness of the other side in this war was proven six years later when a man admitted that he had assassinated Idaho Governor Frank Steunenberg at the direction of the radical union leaders, who had sworn reprisal for Steunenberg's part in breaking the strike. But the victory of the mine owners came long before that sequel, and it was total, except that they often complained later that the replacement miners brought in

Left: *Colonel Isaac N. Peyton was one of three partners of the Le Roi Gold Mine to bring millions of dollars to Spokane. His Peyton Building was constructed in two considerably different styles. In 1898, the Great Eastern Building, on the southeast corner of Riverside Avenue and Post Street, was gutted by fire. Peyton bought the ruins, reinforced the shell, and added two floors. (EWSHS)*

to replace the strikers didn't work as hard.

The mines inevitably changed the character of a little inland town. Those who prospered from the mines by day stood askance at what the mines brought to Spokane streets at night. As the mayor reminded an overzealous police chief in 1897, Spokane was, after all, a mining town, and a certain amount of prostitution and gambling likely would have to be tolerated.

But most of the lasting changes brought by the mines were all to the good. Aside from the mansions, nearly all of which would come into public use, there was a tendency to invest mine earnings in local real estate. In 1898 a group of owners of the Le Roi mine over the Canadian border sold out to Canadian interests for three million dollars. Isaac N. Peyton used his share of the sale to build on the corner of Riverside and Post, and his partner, W.M. Ridpath, invested in a hotel. A third partner, George Turner, the colorful U.S. Senator who sported a bushy black mustache, built the Columbia Building.

The great Hercules Mine, discovered in 1901, added a number of structures to Spokane's cityscape. August Paulsen was a young Swedish immigrant who drifted across the country in the 1890s. He found his way to Spokane, and from there to Burke, Idaho, where he took a job on a dairy farm. He met a young railroad engineer by the name of Levi Hutton and Hutton's betrothed, the operator of a Burke boarding house by the name of May Arkwright.

The three joined a half a dozen other equally poor friends to invest in a mine that had been abandoned earlier by savvy investors. They spent portions of their

In 1901 Levi and May Arkwright Hutton recruited a half-dozen people to help them work their Hercules Mine in northern Idaho. This picture at the mine shows (from left): Tom Harwood, Miss Markwell, Jerome Day, May Hutton, Eugene Day, Miss Hadeen, and Myrtle White, who later married August "Gus" Paulsen. Levi "Al" Hutton is on the far right, and Gus Paulsen stands behind them in the lumber pile. (EWSHS)

The varied styles of turn-of-the-century Spokane architecture are vividly portrayed in this early 1910s view of Post Street at First Avenue, looking north. The elaborate clock tower at the near left is that of the Davenport Restaurant. The Auditorium Theater stands in the left background. The Peyton Building is a block down on the right. (EWSHS)

monthly salaries on dynamite and took turns working the mine. They kept it up for eight years with virtually no recompense. Then, in June of 1901, August Paulsen blasted away a curtain of rock in the mine and, when the dust settled, looked upon what proved to be one of the richest silver and lead finds in history, the famous Hercules.

Their partners, the Day brothers, would stay in mining and become one of the most powerful families in the history of Idaho. Paulsen and the Huttons would move to Spokane, each to leave a mark. Paulsen would immediately erect the first building that bears his name and plan the city's first "skyscraper," the Paulsen Medical-Dental Building (though he would die before he saw it finished in 1928). May, an outspoken woman who had a tendency to say "capitalist slave drivers" when she meant her fellow mine owners, went on to a fame independent of her money as a feminist and campaigner for women's suffrage. She and her husband were both orphans as children, and after her death in 1915 her husband created the famous Hutton Settlement a short distance outside Spokane. It was designed to give children without parents as normal a home setting as possible.

The Hercules would be the last major strike in the Coeur d'Alene. Though the residuals of free-flowing gold, silver, and other treasures would last into the twenties, latecomers to Spokane would find that wealth, or even employment, was becoming difficult to come by.

But they continued to come looking nevertheless. Consider just one of these stories. In 1905 a young man who owned a small photographic shop in Lake Placid, New York, spotted a young woman in his shop and fell in love. Her father would not permit marriage unless the young man had more to offer than the security of a small shop. Specifically, the father said he would be impressed if, within one year, the young man could fulfill three conditions: (a) own a house, (b) have a bank account of $1,000, and (c) be earning $125 a month, a huge salary for that day.

A friend told the young man that Spokane was a likely place to begin, so he rode the train there and took a job as a salesman in the McGowen Brothers Hardware Store at Sprague and Wall. He worked twelve-hour days selling major hardware equipment and was soon making the required salary. After two years he had saved the $1,000 and had begun building a large house at S1115 Grand Avenue. He returned to New York, married the girl, brought her back to Spokane, and lived happily ever after as Henry J. Kaiser, one of the great industrialists of the twentieth century.

Spokane still had the touch.

IV

◆ FRAGMENTS OF LIFE ◆

Spokane had gone from frontier town to boom town to mining town to the gilded residence of millionaires in four quick decades. This burst of activity and wealth produced a city totally different from the Spokane of subsequent decades. Spokane had street lights before San Francisco and Portland. The Auditorium had the largest stage in the West outside of San Francisco and ranked as one of the finer theaters in the country. The Monroe Street Bridge was the longest concrete span in the country when it was completed in 1911, and the third longest in the world. For a few years in the early twenties Hollywood set up shop in Minnehaha Park and the beautiful actress Nell Shipman made a series of movies there.

Things happened during that period which are not likely to be repeated. The Davenport Hotel is the outstanding example. To produce such a building, Kirtland Cutter's talent and twenty years of experience building mansions, the perfectionism of Louis Davenport, and the availability of easy millions, all had to come together at a given time.

Davenport, who had already worked a small pancake house he started in 1889 into the city's finest restaurant, had the curious ambition of operating one of the nation's best hotels in Spokane. As unlikely as it seemed, the hotel he opened in 1914 achieved just that. A special plumbing system brought ice-cold drinking water to every room. The hotel's soda fountain made its own ice cream every day with imported chocolate and fresh strawberries. Employees were given a course in the subtleties of "body language" (as it would be termed decades later) so they would not even unconsciously offend guests. In winter months the fireplace in the lobby was kept blazing around the clock, a job which required the nearly full-time work of a man on each shift. (It was in front of this fire between 1924 and 1929 that one could see Vachel Lindsay, one of America's best poets, sitting in a winged chair, enveloped in a creative daze. He had been lured to Spokane by a local admirer, and Davenport gave him the use of a large suite in the hotel at a bargain price).

Louis Davenport wrote articles on his philosophy of running a hotel and through them influenced the industry. Ernie Pyle, a nationally syndicated columnist in the 1930s and forties, was writing about a more famous hotel in 1939 when he said: "The St. Francis Hotel every night washed all the silver money it had taken in that day—did it in a whirling machine with washing powder and BB shot. The money came out looking as if it had just been minted. They said the idea originated at the Davenport Hotel in Spokane." In Louis Davenport, Kirtland Cutter (by this time known throughout the Northwest for his work) had found the perfect client, one who always put quality above cost.

Not all of the changes brought to Spokane by its surge of growth were beautiful. It was in this era that the river that had given the city its start was virtually lost to it. The city's railroad depot, Union Station, began to take over the riverfront in 1908. By the time it opened

Facing page: *Before the advent of self-service supermarkets, farmers from outlying areas brought their wares downtown to sell directly to the consumer. Horse-drawn wagons crowded together at the farmer's market, on the south side of Second Avenue between Stevens and Washington streets, in this circa 1910 photograph. (EWSHS)*

The Davenport Hotel, designed by architect Kirtland Cutter, attracted celebrities and royalty from the world over. The lobby's lavish decor included tropical plants, singing birds, and glass pillars filled with swimming fish. (EWSHS)

in 1914, a row of tracks, and later trestles raised on riveted black steel pillars, virtually sealed the city off from the river. Jimmy Glover's Front Avenue became the city's back entrance. The graceful Monroe Street Bridge was completed in 1911, but that same year it was marred by a shapeless rail bridge that passed directly over it to bring Union Pacific trains to Havermale Island.

Ugly though these changes may have been, the prominence of the railroads in the city was not out of proportion to their importance to it. Spokane had become a major railroad town, with five of the eight transcontinental railroads coming through the city. On a given day in the 1920s, over 100 trains would roll through the city. Little wonder that, to generations of children who lay in bed trying to sleep, the train's distant, unfolding wail was as familiar as the sound of rain on the window. The trains loaded and unloaded in Spokane twenty-four hours a day and then treaded their way through hills, grass fields, along rivers and to lonely depots a block off the main street of some 500 little communities scattered around the region.

To a growing proportion of the passengers on those trains, Spokane was becoming just another of those lonely stopovers on the way to someplace else. At the turn of the century the Paulsens, Peytons,

Huttons and Ridpaths—Spokane owners of the great mines—began selling out to the John D. Rockefellers, J.P. Morgans and Jay Goulds, Easterners who would spend and invest their profits elsewhere. At the same time, towns in Idaho like Mullen and Wallace were growing enough to draw away some of the mining supply and entertainment functions Spokane had served. Mining money would always be important to Spokane, but after 1900 it would be split up many more ways.

That other indispensible client for Spokane's services, agriculture, was growing more productive all the time as steam and gasoline engines revolutionized wheat farming. Yet the odd economics of agriculture kept a lid on prosperity. Bad growing years hurt farmers, while good ones produced an oversupply which drove down prices and hurt them almost as much. World War I (which did little for Spokane directly, since most war supplies were produced in places where transportation was less of a problem) pushed up the prices of farm products. But with the end of the war, prices plunged again. A bushel of wheat that sold for $2.50 in 1918 sold for only ninety cents in 1922.

Spokane had been prevented from developing a larger manufacturing base by the price policies of the railroads. It cost a Spokane business just about twice as much to ship raw goods from back East as it did a Seattle business, even though the Seattle goods had to travel even further. The difference was that the railroads had a monopoly in Spokane and other inland cities, while in coastal cities rail transport had to compete with ocean

Above: *Two days after the 1889 fire, Louis M. Davenport started "Davenport's Famous Waffle Foundry" in a tent with only 125 dollars. Within a year, Davenport was operating out of a new restaurant that would indeed become famous. In 1914, Davenport opened the three million dollar hotel that would bring the greatest fame to designer Kirtland Cutter. (EWSHS)*

Left: *When the third and present Monroe Street Bridge was constructed, it was the nation's longest and highest concrete span. (EWSHS)*

Above: *Sacred Heart, Spokane's first hospital, was a three-story brick building at the edge of the river, just east of the town center. It was the beginning of a tradition, as Sacred Heart and Deaconess hospitals made Spokane a medical center for an immense area covering four states and part of Canada. The hospital was rebuilt at Eighth Avenue and Browne Street in 1910, as shown here. (EWSHS)*

Right: *The Fox Theater, opened in 1931, was one of the last examples of fine Art Deco architecture in Spokane. The theater was the first built exclusively for moving pictures. (EWSHS)*

transport. The Interstate Commerce Commission, which had been lobbied for two decades by Spokane leaders, finally forced the railroads to standardize their rates in 1918. But in the meantime Spokane manufacturing, wholesaling, and retailing had developed under a heavy disadvantage.

All of these things took their toll, and in the second decade of the century Spokane had lost its status as a wealthy boomtown as suddenly as it had acquired it. By the time state prohibition shut Dutch Jake down in 1916 the excitement was over anyway, and he contentedly turned to serving malteds and colas to ladies and little girls at his bar. Kirtland Cutter finished up his plans for the Chronicle Building and moved to Southern California, where there was still money to build mansions. The Paulsen Medical-Dental Building (1928) was a final donation of the mines, and out-of-town money built the Fox Theater (1931). The emergence of a mass consumer market in the 1920s brought a new Montgomery Ward building and a new Sears Roebuck building in the summer of 1929 (eventually the former would become city hall and the latter the main branch of the public library). A population which had soared from 37,000 at the turn of the century to 100,000 before World War I would grow only another 20,000 until World War II. In 1931, on the occasion of the city's fiftieth anniversary, the president of Whitman College tried to get the city's assembled leaders to imagine Spokane's bright future. "Perhaps it will shock you," he told them, "if I suggest that fifty years from now not one of the buildings which line your streets will be standing." What really would have shocked them would have been if the speaker had guessed that forty years later *all* the same buildings would still be standing; that for four decades there would be almost no improvements to Spokane's downtown area.

In most books, pamphlets, articles, and dissertations about Spokane's past, the final passages describe the sale of the big mines and history draws to a close about 1920. Of course, to people who lived in Spokane in the subsequent decades it didn't seem that way. Life—real, everyday life—went on.

History has a pattern, that checkerboard of events and intertwining causes which we study to extract lessons. Like the pattern in a quilt, it is what we see when we stand off at some distance and

Above: *The Great Northern Railroad was the first to lay track along the Spokane riverfront and Havermale Island, in 1901. By the time this picture was taken, in 1924, the railroads had overrun the island and south bank. (EWSHS)*

Above, left: *The soil of the hills to the south and west of Spokane would prove to be the most enduring source of wealth for the Inland Empire, but clearing it of bunch grass and bringing in those early crops was arduous work. This circa 1915 picture was taken on the farm of John A. Fancher, a pioneer who settled near Deep Creek southwest of Spokane in the 1870s. (EWSHS)*

Above: *The Spokane-Coeur d'Alene interurban electric railway made regular stops at Liberty Lake starting in 1910. By the summer of 1913, special trains were leaving Spokane every few minutes to bring thousands of swimmers, bathers, and picnickers to the most popular of the area's lakes. (EWSHS)*

Right: *A popular turn-of-the-century outing included an interurban train ride to Coeur d'Alene, followed by a steamboat excursion around the lake and up the St. Joe River. (EWSHS)*

Left: *Ingersall's Park, a large field at the west end of Boone Avenue, was a popular picnic and baseball spot for Spokanites as early as the mid-1880s. In 1909 Washington Water Power converted it into the Natatorium Park amusement area as an incentive for riders to use its Monroe-Boone railway line. Some of the later attractions of Nat Park included the "Jack Rabbit" roller-coaster, the airplane ride, "Dodg'em" bumper cars, and the famous merry-go-round. It has been estimated that over four million people rode the merry-go-round while at Nat Park. In 1967 the Nat Park amusements were dismantled to make way for the San Souci West Mobile Park. The merry-go-round is now preserved at Riverfront Park. (EWSHS)*

These kids in the 1920s are getting a thrill on the "Jack Rabbit." (EWSHS)

Bobsledders enjoy the steepness of Howard Street near Seventh Avenue, in the winter of 1890-1891. The large building in the right background is the Spokesman-Review Building before its tower was added the following year. (EWSHS)

look. But history also has a texture: the way it actually felt to those who touched it. Unfortunately museums cannot preserve, alongside their fragments of history—letters, weapons, clothing, utensils—these fragments of life: the feeling of a favorite coat to a particular woman on a particular evening in her life; the back yard on a warm summer afternoon as experienced by a twelve-year-old boy or girl. For most people most of the time, these evanescent moments are what the past really was. One's hometown, by providing the weather, the sounds, the diversions, the tempo of life, has much to do with fixing this texture.

What constituted the texture of life in Spokane? Surely the lakes were an important part of it. Roger Anderson, a city councilman in the 1970s who had moved to Spokane from the west side of the state, once observed that when he first arrived he was puzzled to hear people say they were going to "the lake," as if there were only one. The Spokane expression—which refers to lakes as a universally understood experience rather than a specific place—suggests the role played by the seventy-six lakes within commuting distance of Spokane. By 1902 electric trains were leaving Spokane daily to take people all the way to Lake Coeur d'Alene. In the opposite direction, little Medical Lake enjoyed a sudden popularity when it was supposed that the murky water had curative powers. A full-fledged resort drew hundreds of swimmers on a weekend.

Liberty Lake, being the nearest at hand, was the most popular at the turn of the century and through the 1920s. Developers built a resort hotel and a dance hall on pilings out over the water. When the sun finally went down on a summer night, fireworks often lit up the sky and a steamboat pulled a floating dance floor around the lake. By 1911, trains on Sundays and holidays would deliver five cars full of picnickers every hour. Every company, school, lodge and nationality had its annual picnic, with fried chicken, watermelon, soda and kegs of beer. The biggest crowd ever recorded at Liberty was that of July 4, 1924, when an estimated 14,000 people stepped over each other trying to get to the water.

About that time automobiles and better highways began dispersing the crowds to more lakes. But the essential experience of the lake—long summer days, the sun hanging motionless in the sky, the drone of voices on the water, the rattle of the diving board and the sound of the plunge—would remain the same in 1980 as it was in 1940 and 1920 and even 1902.

Almost as redolent with memory, at least to anyone who was born prior to 1950 or so, was Natatorium Park, a strange assortment of mammoth machinery arranged along the lower Spokane River for the purpose of selling thrills to the crowds which swarmed its lawns and pathways on sunny afternoons. It was constructed in 1887 as an incentive to use the new cable line that traveled to it via west Boone Avenue. Rides were added every year—the Tunnel of Love, the Shoot-the-Shoots, the Jack Rabbit—until it became the major diversion of pre-television decades. Its finest piece by far was the merry-go-round, carved in hardwood by the now famous Charles I. Looff of New York City. It came to Spokane in 1911 as part of a deal that allowed Looff's new son-in-law to become a partner in the amusement park. When the park was closed in the 1960s, the merry-go-round (now called the Carousel) was saved and eventually re-erected in Riverfront Park.

As the city's first park board president and "civic development" writer for the Spokesman-Review, *Aubrey L. White campaigned twenty-six years to beautify the city and develop parks. White was responsible for securing the undeveloped land for Riverside State Park, Mt. Spokane State Park, and Deep Creek Canyon, to name a few. (EWSHS)*

The three decades following 1920 were the era of the park. Manito Park, which housed the city zoo until it was closed in 1933, drew visitors from all over the city by way of the trolley that rattled and clanged its way up Grand Boulevard. It was almost as popular in winter as in summer because of its sledding hills and large skating pond. Most parks in the city had skating ponds in the winter, even if they were only tennis courts flooded by the city park department. In contention with a day at the lake for the most common association with "growing up in Spokane" would be one of white landscapes and blue winter evenings, the muffled click of ice skates, the vague scent of wood and coal smoke mingling in the fresh cold air.

Spokane acquired its national award-winning park system largely through the personal efforts of a man by the name of Aubrey L. White. White had come to Spokane from Maine in 1889 at the age of twenty. He was sent back East in 1896 to sell mining stocks in New York City, and there for ten years he viewed first-

Above: *This photo of the Musicaladers appeared in an advertisement for Lareida's Dance Pavilion in the Spokane Valley. Courtesy, George Lareida, Jr.*

Right: *"Field Day" attracted hundreds of spectators to the quarter-mile horse and bicycle track at Corbin Park, near Cleveland Avenue and Howard Street. People all over Spokane hopped onto streetcars to come to Corbin Park for a day of band concerts, leisurely walks, and the races. (EWSHS)*

Above: *Many Spokane couples danced across this floor at Whitehead's Dance Palace in the 1920s. (EWSHS)*

Above left: *The young Bing Crosby often came to Whitehead's on West 313 Sprague Avenue to listen to the music of the Jazz Age. (EWSHS)*

hand both what an urban area can be like without parks and the complications of trying to create parks after an area has already been developed.

When he returned to Spokane to find it booming and headed for exactly those same problems, White organized his powerful mining acquaintances behind a campaign to change the city charter. His aim was to set up a park board independent of the city council. The charter amendment passed, and White became the reconstituted park board's first president in 1907. His first action was to hire as consultants the Olmsted brothers of Massachusetts, designers of dozens of urban park systems, including New York City's Central Park.

The report prepared by the Olmsteds was bold. Even as Union Station was being constructed, the report pointed out what a mistake it was to spoil the river's natural beauty like this. The report also said Spokane needed five times as much park space as it had.

The Olmsted recommendations became Aubrey White's marching orders. He laid the city map before him and concocted strategies to take prize pieces of land, along the river and throughout the city. When he ran into serious obstacles he would gather a select group of backers—William H. Cowles, Sr., John Finch, Louis Davenport and Joel Ferris—for a luncheon and a solicitation. What was not donated one way or another was purchased with part of a one-million-dollar bond issue White got voters to approve in 1910. By the time White left the park board in 1921 most of the city's park system had been assembled.

A small fraction of the work White did for Spokane was leading the park board to plant 80,000 trees along its streets, and encouraging citizens to add more. His friend and supporter, millionaire developer Jay P. Graves, planted the trees along Grand Boulevard. Among the trees planted under White's supervision between 1910 and 1920 are the very ones that still shade Riverside Avenue west of Monroe, Mission Avenue, and numerous other streets.

Behind those trees were built, from about 1900 to 1930, the big, bulky family houses of Spokane's close-in neighborhoods. Visitors often find these well-preserved neighborhoods—ranging from the stately homes opposite the Cheney Cowles Museum to the plain, box-like houses of Peaceful Valley just over the bluff—the most fascinating part of Spokane.

It's entirely appropriate that it was a Spokane woman, Mrs. John Bruce Dodd, who in 1910 originated the observance of Father's Day. This is when Spokane was making the radical transition from boomtown to "a nice place to raise a family." That was the reason that Harry Lowe Crosby gave for moving his family from Tacoma to Spokane in 1906. The most remarkable thing about Bing Crosby's childhood in Spokane is that there was so little remarkable about it. He swam at Mission pool, delivered the *Spokesman-Review,* loved playing baseball and pranks, got in the requisite number of fistfights, and couldn't sing all that well. He was the typical Spokane kid. The family, mom and dad and seven children, lived in a big yellow house at E508 Sharp, one block from the entrance to Gonzaga University. Bing attended Webster Grade School and Gonzaga High School before he entered Gonzaga's law school. He had dreams of becoming a great trial lawyer, but those apparently bogged down amid the profusely footnoted statutes.

The talent that everyone who knew Bing in Spokane remembers is not his singing but his witty tongue. George Lareida, who hired Crosby's band, has said that when you see him in the "Road" pictures trading quips with Bob Hope, "that's the fellow he was." Arthur Dussault, S.J., a chum of Bing's, remembers working out with the Gonzaga basketball team while Bing, typically, provided from the sidelines an unsolicited, needling, but funny commentary on the action.

When Bing started performing, it was as a second-rate drummer in a band that did mostly instrumentals. The band, called the Musicaladers, booked minor dances and restaurants around town. None of its members had much musical training. They built up a repertoire by going to Baily's record store near the northwest corner of Riverside and Post and crowding into the booths to listen to a record over and over until each band member had his part memorized.

The winter of 1925-1926 they played at Lareida's, a former automobile display room on the 4900 block of East Sprague which had been transformed into a popular dance hall. On a bandstand in the middle of the floor, sitting behind a bass drum decorated with a Japanese painting of a sunset, hundreds of Spokanites of the "Jazz Age" saw Crosby perform over the winter of 1925 and 1926. The Musicaladers had to be inventive to fill a whole evening with the few songs they were able to memorize. They would take a waltz and play it as a foxtrot, or copy the Dixieland style. At intervals Bing would step forward for some somber lowing about losing the one you loved, or with a livelier tune of the day.

That spring Bing and Al Rinker, the talented piano player who had started the Musicaladers, landed a job doing musical warm-ups to silent movies at what was then known as the Clemmer Theater (now the State Theater), at the corner of Sprague and Lincoln. Here they began to polish the little act—Rinker at the piano singing along as Bing warbled and joked through a brief medley of songs—that would take them both to fame a few years later.

After the show Bing usually went to

When Norma Talmadge and the cast of "Smiling Through" posed in front of the Liberty Theater in the early 1920s, downtown Spokane had no less than fifteen theaters. The Liberty, located at West 716 Riverside Avenue, was considered the *downtown picture house, competing with the Clemmer, until the Fox was built in 1931. The Liberty seated 1,000 people, and is credited with running the first sound movies in town. The theater was remodeled into Lerner's Dress Shop in 1953. (EWSHS)*

Stubeck's confectionery, on the northwest corner of Sprague and Wall, a hangout for young people of that time, or up the street to Whitehead's dance hall where he could listen to other bands play. This was the major gathering place during Spokane's roaring twenties.

It was outside Whitehead's that Dutch Groshoff, a friend of Bing's and a well-known Spokane musician, came upon Bing about midnight one night. Bing, still dressed in his striped jacket and bowler hat, was handcuffed to a policeman who was arresting him for possessing bootleg liquor. As the policeman requested a paddy wagon from a nearby callbox, a small crowd from the dance hall gathered and appealed to the cop to let Bing go "this time." When the paddy wagon arrived, the policeman opened the rear doors, climbed in, and pulled Bing up after him. As Bing stepped up, he turned, doffed his bowler hat with his free hand, and executed a grand bow to the crowd. The policeman jerked the handcuffs and Bing disappeared into the dark wagon.

Later that spring Father Dussault found Bing in a vacant lot behind the Crosby house and across the street from Gonzaga tinkering with an ancient automobile. Bing told him he and Rinker had purchased the car and were going to use it to blow this burg—go to the big time. That was a familiar refrain among Spokane kids in these decades when there was little economic growth to provide jobs for all the children growing up in the large families of the era. Dussault advised Bing to at least finish out the semester of law school—just in case he didn't become a big Hollywood star.

On the appointed morning Rinker showed up at the Crosby house and was amazed to find Bing still slumbering peacefully. The two loaded Bing's drums in the back of the old car, said goodbye to the Crosby family, and pulled away from the curb. They drove down to Stitz' gas station at Boone and Division, where a friend gave them a fill-up and agreed to catch them later for the money. Then Bing put the flivver into gear and started south on Division.

Anyone who turned to look at them pass by would have witnessed an historic moment: Bing Crosby on the road to Hollywood. Or so it seems to us now, in retrospect, with the whole pattern of his subsequent success in place. At the time it was just another few moments of "now," another fragment of life. To a couple of Spokane boys putt-putting toward the Division Street Bridge on a brisk spring morning it was just "today."

V

◆ The Wide World Impinges ◆

A person sitting down with a cup of coffee and the *Spokesman-Review* the morning of October 24, 1929 would have the future in front of him, if only he could know how to decipher the hints. A cartoon on the front page joked that railroad service was soon going to decline to the point where people would find it easier to take a bus, or even an *airplane!* Page two of that morning's paper told the reader: "Theoretically, it is possible to transmit the image of a man making a speech, while the radio carries the voice. Ultimately, you may be able to sit beside your receiving set and watch a football game in progress while the announcer gives the running account of the game." A few pages further on, an editorial noted the continuing squabbles between France and Germany and was thankful that President Wilson had not been able to get the United States in the League of Nations at the end of World War I.

But the big headline of that day read: "Cataclysm Hits Stocks In Hour . . . Prices Flatten Out Like Punctured Balloon." If the reader was an investor in the stock market, as millions of ordinary people were in 1929, he had to be concerned. But no matter how shocked our reader, he could hardly have suspected, as he finished his coffee and stepped outside to a clear, 65-degree day, that everything was about to change. Whatever he had planned for the future, and whatever the community had planned for its future, it was all changed now. For the next sixteen years Spokane was at the mercy of larger forces, like a cardboard box tossed and flipped in a hurricane.

Facing page: *Newsboys like E.A. Cahill, shown here in 1924, shouted out the day's headlines each evening as people headed for the trolley and their Model Ts. The newsboys' chants were a part of the fabric of life in the 1920s and 1930s. (EWSHS)*

The effects of the stock market crash and ensuing economic chaos were gradual but relentless. The city's loss of economic momentum is reflected in the steady fall of the value of the construction undertaken. From $4.1 million in 1929, Spokane building permits fell to $3.6 million in 1930, $2 million in 1931, and finally bottomed out at the standstill level of $572,000 in 1932.

The Farmers and Merchants Bank closed in November of 1931, and the Wall Street, State and American Banks closed a few months later. Rumors swirled around the fate of the Old National Bank, the epitome of financial security and holder of one out of four accounts in the region. It closed with the national "bank holiday" on March 2, 1933 and didn't reopen until October 9 of that year, at which time depositors were allowed to claim up to 40 percent of their deposits.

Spending during Christmas of 1932 was half what it had been three years earlier. Two large department stores, Culbertsons and the Palace, were among the dozens of businesses which collapsed under the financial pressures. At the depth of the Depression in 1932, only one in seven street-level addresses along Riverside were vacant. But one in four of them had either been under new ownership since 1929 or were completely new businesses.

Unable to collect property taxes, city government cut its 1932 budget by 20 percent. One of the things cut was the zoo in Manito Park. The parks director could not even give away the animals to another city, so several of them, including two grizzly bears and a polar bear, were killed and stuffed to be placed in the city's museum.

Approximately one out of four of all Spokane workers were without jobs, including many who headed families. Very few could get county relief money, so they borrowed or they simply went hungry. Others jumped aboard railroad trains and began to drift from place to place, as people all over the country were doing. Boxcars draped with hundreds of people—men, women and children—were a common sight in Spokane. So many drifters arrived in Spokane that the city government established a transient hotel that could house up to 600 people a day. These transients were allowed to stay up to thirty days and then were forced to leave town.

Dr. Alexander Barclay of Coeur d' Alene abolished all debts owed him for Christmas of 1932, saying, "I believe that this should be done generally, as far as possible, all along the line, if people are to retain their courage to continue to battle for their homes and families. The suicide list is growing appallingly and the spectres of debt, want and misery are stalking the land with Seven League Boots. Peace on earth, good will to men."

The emergency relief programs of the Roosevelt administration began to take hold early in 1934. That year the heads of 6,000 Spokane families received federal paychecks. They were paid for their civic

The Lincoln Statue, sculpted by Alfonzo Victor Lewis of Seattle, was dedicated November 11, 1930, at a spot about thirty feet south of its present position. Films of the dedication show a time capsule placed in the base of this statue. Although there is no record of its contents, the capsule would surely reflect the last moments of innocence in Spokane. (EWSHS)

This aerial view of the downtown business district was taken in 1931. While the valley and surrounding areas would undergo drastic expansion, downtown Spokane would change little in the next thirty-five years. (EWSHS)

C.E. Marr established the first self-service grocery store in Spokane in 1918. Prior to the opening of Marr's Store Number Two on Riverside Avenue, east of Lincoln Street, shoppers read a grocery list to a store clerk, who ran back and forth plucking the items from the shelves. By 1921 there would be thirty "Marr's Help Yourself Stores" in Spokane and they would be a familiar part of daily life in every part of town. Marr's grocery chain eventually evolved into Piggly-Wiggly's and Safeway. (EWSHS)

Right: *The Salvation Army's headquarters on Main Avenue east of Bernard Street fed thousands of people who wandered through Spokane during the Depression. (EWSHS)*

Below: *Spokane's passion for fairs began with the Washington and Idaho Fair, October 1887, evolving into the "Spokane Interstate Fair" in August 1901. The Depression ended the fair in 1930. The fair was not to revive until 1952. (EWSHS)*

work and, though the purpose was to feed families, the city got some important work done in these years at bargain prices. Crews on federal relief payrolls put in fifty-five miles of sewers, virtually completing the city system. Others graded streets, rebuilt the Felts Field airport and renovated many of the city's schools. White collar workers did everything from indexing the local newspapers to teaching night classes offered free to the public. Crews of the Civilian Conservation Corps, a federal program that brought young men here from all over the country, built many of the campgrounds and roads still in use in forested areas of the region.

One of the largest of all Roosevelt programs, and in fact one of the largest construction programs in the history of the world, was proceeding just seventy-five miles west of Spokane. Grand Coulee Dam would change the history of the state and Spokane by irrigating tens of thousands of acres of land and making industrial and private energy cheaper in Spokane than in any other place in the country.

Partly as a result of federal programs, the economy began to recover quickly af-

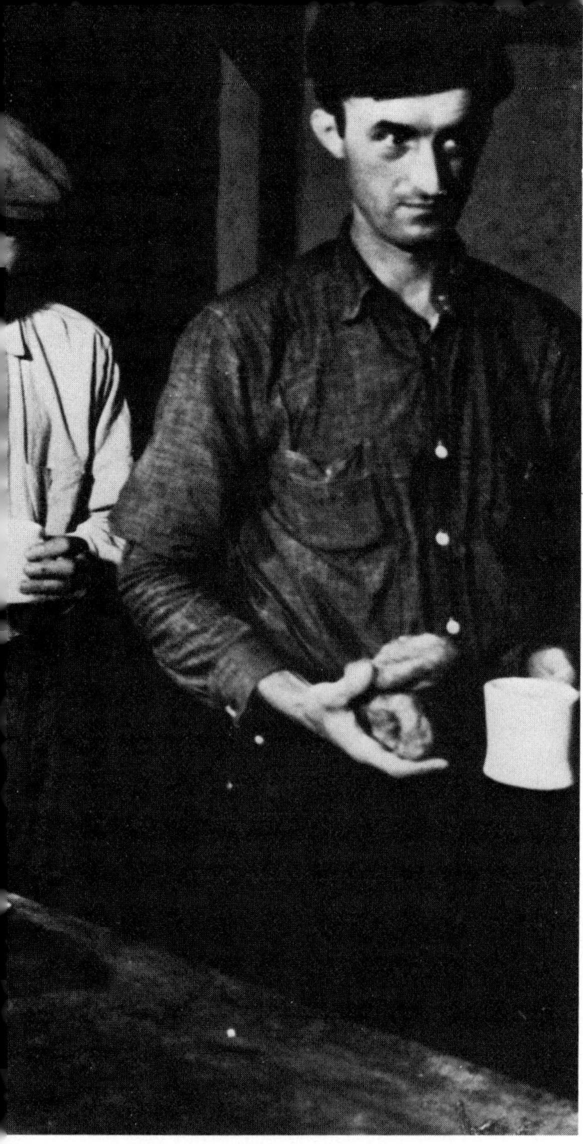

President Franklin D. Roosevelt, flanked by his sons John and James and Washington Senator Clarence C. Dill, left, waved goodbye as his train left the Ephata Great Northern station, following his first visit to the Grand Coulee Dam site, August 7, 1934. The construction of Grand Coulee Dam, for decades the world's largest dam, changed Northwest history by using inexpensive power to draw aluminum and other industries, and by irrigating thousands of acres of previously dry farmland. Senator Dill, a Spokanite, was an early Roosevelt supporter, and was instrumental in winning presidential support for the Columbia River project. (EWSHS)

ter 1937. By Christmas of 1939, spending in downtown department stores finally returned to what it had been in 1929. Seven days later the Depression decade was happily forgotten in parties at the Davenport Hotel, Spokane Club, and many other places around the city.

To many people and in varying degrees, the thirties had been idle, drab, impoverishing, humiliating, and horrible. The first half of the coming decade would prove frenetic, vivid, prosperous, glorious—and to many equally horrible.

December 7, 1941 was a sunny winter day in Spokane, with temperatures in the forties. Many people heard the news of the bombing of Pearl Harbor on their car radios as they drove home from church that morning. Others stopped what they were doing at home and turned the radio up loud to listen to the reports. Many people remember getting phone calls from excited relatives. What did it mean? It was one of those rare times in life when every single person in a community had a clear sense that his or her life was going to change.

In the days immediately following Pearl Harbor, lines formed at local recruiting stations and the Armory was swamped by enlistees and draftees lining up for physicals. John Matsch, forty-two years old and a veteran of World War I, was at the recruiting office December 8, 1941, trying to get back into the Navy. He finally wrangled his way in six months later on the basis of his technical skills from the last war. In the process, one of the recruiters he had badgered said, "Why don't you just wait? This thing is going to last a long time and we'll come looking for you sooner or later." It was a long war. Toward the end men in their late thirties and men with several children were being fitted for uniforms so that they could replace the teenagers who had gone in the beginning.

Approximately 15,000 people from Spokane County were in the armed forces during World War II. Ask anyone born before about 1925 where he or she was on a given date between 1942 and 1945 and you are as likely to hear "Burma" or "Tarawa," "Salerno," "Normandy" or "Berlin" as you are "Spokane." It was as if the city had shattered with Pearl Harbor, scattering its pieces to every corner of the earth.

Dozens of Spokane men were killed or taken captive in the initial Japanese attacks on Pacific islands. Among them were Sammy Gracio, the pilot who would become the city's first hero by escaping from a prisoner of war camp, and Lloyd Catlow, a Marine who was one of the last Corregidor holdouts to be captured.

Spokane was the home of two major reserve units at the outset of the war. The 161st Infantry Regiment of the Washington National Guard, which drew rifle companies from throughout eastern Washington, would fight through Okinawa and Luzon and eventually take part in the occupation of Japan.

The 14th Marine Corps Reserve battalion, also based in Spokane, was called into active service a year before the outset of the war. Thc unit was divided up and its members scattered throughout the Pacific.

Among them were six boyhood friends who had enlisted in the unit together in 1938: Jack Burke of Gonzaga High School; Bill Higgins of Lewis and Clark High School; Oliver Hauschild of North Central High; Bud Womble of Rogers; Ray Morse of North Central; and Phil Baldwin of North Central. Their fates are a snapshot of the war in the Pacific. Burke was a bombardier on a torpedo plane and was killed shortly after Pearl Harbor when his plane went down in the Pacific. Higgins was taken prisoner by the Japanese at Guam. Hauschild and Womble were both wounded at Guadalcanal, the first step in the American counter-offensive. Morse was one of the defenders of Midway when the Japanese were thwarted in their attempt to invade by the sudden arrival of the American fleet. Baldwin was one of the 4,500 Americans killed at Iwo Jima at the doorstep of Japan in 1945.

In the first year of the war defense installations began to fringe the city like modern ramparts. This was a war of *materiel,* and Spokane shipped off hundreds of thousands of tons of it. To the north and east of the city (separated in case of a bombing attack) were the federal government's aluminum mills. Also in the valley was the Velox Naval Supply Depot, opened January 1, 1943. In its twenty-nine large warehouses (which would become the Spokane Industrial Park after the war) it stored: 110,000 galvanized buckets; 2,500 sixty-man life rafts; 137,000 hospital blankets; 7 million bottles of insect repellent; 660,000 pounds of medicated cotton; 300 train carloads of Navy clothing; and countless other items which would have to be disbursed around the world before the war was won.

To the city's southwest was a much larger operation, the Army Air Corps supply and repair depot known as Galena. It was one of four such installations in the country and had been vigorously courted by the Chamber of Commerce in the years just prior to the war. Galena served as a kind of giant pit stop for bombers. A damaged or worn plane would land on its criss-crossing airstrips and head for a cavernous hangar that covered eleven acres of ground. In a period of three or four days, crews working around the clock would have gone over every rivet and bolt, in essence turning out a new plane. In its two years of operation more than 10,000 airplane engines were repaired at the depot.

At the city's west gate was the venerable Fort George Wright. Just prior to the outbreak of World War II it had exchanged the last of its old army mules and horses for mechanized transportation. For awhile it was an Air Corps headquarters—the one to which Lieutenant Clark Gable reported on January 10, 1943. (The star of *Gone With The Wind,* which premiered at the Fox Theater April 18, 1940, was a distraction because secretaries all over the post kept finding excuses to go through his office). Toward the end of the war the fort became a convalescent hospital.

To the northwest of the city (on the site of the present Veterans Hospital) was Baxter Army Hospital. The injured came to it in caravans from all over the world. On one particular day it admitted 256 patients; by May 5, 1945—two days prior to victory in Europe and three months before victory in Japan—it had logged 10,000 patients.

The mood of the city was combative. No matter what the losses suffered by Americans, newspaper stories always took a "you should have seen the other guy" slant. People returning from the front were interviewed, sent to high school convocations and paraded through downtown. A big military parade on July 22, 1944, had appropriately attired clowns with signs around their necks reading "Adolf," "Benito" and "Tojo" being pulled along by ropes around their necks.

In one sense there were few places on the face of the earth more remote from the war than Spokane. But in another sense every battle cast its shadows across the city. At the sight of a Western Union boy riding down the street, people would drop what they were doing and hold their breath; if he stopped, their lives might change forever.

When her nineteen-year-old son got his wings in the Army Air Corps, Mrs. Helen Mangan, the wife of a Spokane police sergeant, wrote a poem:

Dear God, it seems but yesterday
you gave this son to me.
The one who's miles from
home
Whose face I cannot see.
The years have swiftly come and gone,
So eager in their stride
To brush me lightly by the way,
And take him from my side.
It seems to me he's still a child...

He was killed one year later when his B-17 was shot down in France. Alan Campbell Powell, grandson of Amasa B. Campbell, a bomber pilot as well, was also killed in France. Cheney Cowles, the second son of the *Spokesman-Review* publisher, was killed in a plane crash in the states while training. Captain Jack Miller, the thirty-year-old Princeton-educated grandson of Spokane pioneer and millionaire Patrick Welch, died in the

During the Second World War it was not uncommon to look down a Spokane street and see more people in uniform than in civilian dress. This photo was snapped toward the end of the war, looking east down Sprague Avenue from Lincoln Street. Courtesy, Spokane Magazine

Although every household in the nation was affected to some degree by the war effort, few Spokane-area families suffered more loss than the Bangs. Melvin, Peter, Irene, Sidnie, and John Bang all left their Spokane Valley home to join the armed forces. Melvin and Sidnie died overseas. On this page, clockwise, are Melvin, Irene, and John. Facing page, left to right, are Peter and Sidnie. Courtesy, the Bang family

Soloman Islands. Archie Buckley, the popular head football coach of North Central, was trying to help another man during an attack on their aircraft carrier when he was killed. Private Joe E. Mann of Reardan, after parachuting into the Netherlands in September 1944, was wounded two different times, once in each arm, during fierce close-in fighting. A grenade landed near him but behind other members of the platoon in the bunker. With both arms bandaged to his sides he was unable to throw it, so he yelled to the others and then covered the grenade with his body just as it exploded. He was awarded the Medal of Honor posthumously.

With approximately 15,000 people from Spokane County serving, virtually every family had someone to worry about. Few families had more on the line than the Bang family, which had immigrated from Norway to the Spokane Valley in 1921. Five of eight children were in the service: Sidnie was on a tank destroyer in Europe, John was on a ship in the Pacific, Peter was with the Army in India, Melvin was in the Army Engineers in the Pacific, and Irene was in the Waves in California. Sidnie is buried in Belgium and Melvin is buried in the Philippines.

In all, there were about 500 who did not return to homes in Spokane and the Valley.

It was about 4 p.m. on August 14, a Tuesday, when Spokane got the news that the war was over. As word spread downtown by radio and word-of-mouth, people came streaming out of department

stores and office buildings onto the streets. "For the first few minutes there was little noise," the *Spokesman-Review* reported. "Then automobile horns began to blow. In a few minutes their blasts became a solid wave of sound in downtown streets."

In those first few moments of knowing it was all over a person could hardly do otherwise than review what the war had meant: loneliness; people who would now be coming back; people who wouldn't; friends in foreign lands and tropic jungles; going home. All sorts of emotions exploded on the crowded downtown streets. Next to people laughing and embracing were people crying and being comforted by strangers. Instead of subsiding, the celebration intensified late into the night until downtown streets were clogged by bumper-to-bumper cars and the sidewalks were impassable.

Of course, the end of the war came differently to many other Spokanites. At the northern edge of Japan, in a place so remote that vehicles could not reach it, an American soldier arrived by parachute to tell Sergeant Lloyd Catlow, a Marine captured on Corregidor, and about 200 other American prisoners the news—which they had already guessed when their Japanese guards had suddenly disappeared. Food was dropped in for the following three weeks so the half-starved men, most of whom had been in the deadly camps three years, could build up the strength to walk out.

Catlow returned to Seattle by British and American ships. From there he had the choice of returning to Spokane by train or bus. He chose the bus because he had been thinking for weeks about what it would be like to come down Sunset Hill again and see Spokane. "I had that imprinted on my mind," Catlow remembered later. "I wanted to look down on the city from Sunset Hill." Late one afternoon in the winter of 1945 the bus rolled over the West Plains, reached the crest of the hill, and started down. Catlow leaned close to the bus window and looked. "And there she was, spread out at the bottom of the hill, just like I imagined it."

For many people, the war was over the day they got home.

VI

Coeur D'Alene
HOTEL
HOME OF THE
DUTCH
MILL
1890
BLOCK
VISITING
NURSES
SMARTEST CLOTHES
IN TOWN
ON CREDIT
CAFE
HOTEL
APARTMENTS
Hardware
HOESLYS
HARDWARE

• Spokane Recumbent •

Spokane emerged from the war with a revitalized economy. The twin aluminum plants at Mead and Trentwood were purchased from the federal government by ex-Spokanite Henry J. Kaiser and began supplying the modern metal to civilian markets. The Army Air Depot (renamed Fairchild Air Force Base in 1950) became a permanent installation and added a huge military payroll to the city's economy. The Navy's abandoned Velox Supply Depot, with its neat rows of warehouses on railroad sidings, supplied ready-made housing for dozens of new businesses as the Spokane Industrial Park. Geiger Field, the landing strip begun by the city just prior to the war and completed by the Army Air Corps, was now turned back to the city and Spokane had a modern airport. Each of these new assets produced its offshoots: construction of houses, new businesses (an example was the new fabricators of aluminum products), new stores, and restaurants. Very few of the 10,000 discharged GIs returning to Spokane had trouble finding jobs.

The GI Bill and no-down-payment terms meant almost anyone could buy a house. In 1947 alone there were 2,500 houses built in Spokane, five times as many as any year prior to the war. Fields of wild grass and basalt outcroppings at the north edge of the city were suddenly covered with pastel houses and lawns nursed by hissing sprinklers.

Nineteen-fifty-five was a good year for city housing, with over 2,800 lots platted. But that same year there were twice as many lots platted beyond the city's limits, most of them to the east in the Valley. It wasn't noticed yet, but the city was undergoing profound changes.

After World War II, the faster automobile, improved roads, and cheap gasoline made it possible for the middle class to combine the prosperity and diversions of the city with the pastoral quiet of the country. And land "in the country" was often cheaper than city lots. This and the fact that one did not have to pay for sidewalks, sewers, police protection, and many other expenses of urban life usually made up for the cost of fuel for the commute back and forth.

Bigger populations in the Spokane Valley, which set up demands for better roads (culminating in the completion of the I-90 freeway in 1967), drew still more people to the valley. Meanwhile, the city taxpayer bore the whole cost of maintaining an expensive city core, even though that core was used just as much by many Valley residents. The difference in tax burdens became one more reason to move beyond the city limits.

All of these things set up a kind of centrifugal force that was pulling population, particularly younger and more affluent families, from the city and scattering it about the surrounding environs. In 1940, the Spokane Valley was mostly orchards and small farms and had a total population of 10,000. By 1960 that had increased to 45,000, and by 1970 to 60,000—the population of a medium-sized city.

This separation of the city from a large portion of its population was the cause of two of the most serious crises in Spo-

Facing page: *Spokane of the 1950s was made up of turn-of-the-century buildings modified to meet the needs of a half-century later. The photo shows Bennett Block and Dutch Jake's Coeur d'Alene Hotel. (EWSHS)*

Until the advent of improved roads and automobiles after World War II, Spokane was a tightly packed urban area surrounded by farms barely in view of each other. This was the home of Daniel Meikle of Otis Orchards, circa 1915. (EWSHS)

kane's history. The first was the threat to health when an urban area grew up without the standard urban sewer system. The explosive growth in the valley was nominally under the direction of the government of Spokane County. But a board of three commissioners, formed by the state constitution in the last century mainly to oversee the maintenance of roads and other minor services required by a rural area, was ill-equipped to deal with the complexities of urban development. Essential services like water supply and fire protection were provided by independent districts. But certain things—overall planning for example—cannot be done piecemeal. Neither the traditions of county government nor the personalities of those usually elected to serve in it provided the impetus to take hold of the fast-changing situation.

Among the consequences was that the valley became one of the largest urban areas in the country not served by sewers. The rocky valley soil and substrata happened to be almost perfect for the septic drain field system of sewage disposal. Sewage virtually never saturated the soil and appeared on the surface of the ground, the kind of failure which

In the early 1920s, Spokane citizens authorized the expenditure of $1 million to build a coliseum, but a debate over where it should be located delayed and then ultimately scuttled the idea. The issue was revived after World War II by a group of citizens who put on a successful campaign to finance a coliseum. The 8,000-seat Coliseum, at Boone Avenue and Howard Street, was completed in 1954. Prior to its construction no indoor theater or arena in town would hold more than 1,000 people. (EWSHS)

usually forced a town to begin the expensive process of installing sewers. Unfortunately, the same permeability which allows sewage to move so reliably downward is, at a deeper level, what allows water from mountains and lakes of Idaho to flow underground to Spokane, supplying the city's drinking water. If the two—the valley sewage and the water in the underground aquifer—should begin to mingle, one of the finest natural water supply systems in the world would be tainted.

In the early 1960s a consultant told the county that pollutants probably were not reaching the aquifer. In the early seventies new studies indicated they probably were. But in the early 1980s the county took the first steps toward building a valley sewer system. Presumably the city's irreplaceable water supply finally would be safeguarded.

The second threat of the postwar move to the suburbs was to Spokane's downtown. The people who now found shopping at a nearby shopping center much more convenient were the same people who had been supporting downtown restaurants, theaters, and other attractions. The loss of the retail shopper had made many American city centers compounds of business and professional offices which on a weekend showed hardly a sign of life, something not quite a city, something perfectly described by Gertrude Stein when she said of Oakland: "There's no *there* there."

In Spokane this nationwide trend toward the desertion of the city core was one more burden in a time of general decline. After the initial boom of World War II and the years immediately following, the city's economy began to slide again. In one disastrous year (1957), the wood products industry went into a slump, Kaiser Aluminum reduced its operations, and the Air Force moved units of fighter planes from their base at Geiger Field. Many other businesses and regional offices were closed about this time, and one study indicated that between 1957 and 1963 the city had lost six percent of its jobs. A study of the fifties and early sixties by Gonzaga University said: "The Spokane economy, contrary to bright reports in the local media, was not making very great progress. In fact our data indicated that Spokane was nearly standing still relative to itself and was falling behind in comparison to other areas."

The city's malaise was apparent every-

The Parkade is a landmark of Spokane's renaissance. Its construction in 1966 was the beginning of the city's decade of downtown renewal. The second-floor skywalk was initiated with the Parkade. The first skywalks, shown here, were arched concrete walkways with plastic-covered canopies. The alley behind the Parkade and Fidelity Bank Building was converted into an open plaza. (EWSHS)

where. Many downtown addresses were vacant. The public face of the city, its city hall, was a weary, clanking six-story building with the general demeanor of a jailhouse. Perhaps the perfect symbol of neglect was the condition of the city's major physical attraction and distinction, the river. Though the state director of health had certified the Spokane River as a health hazard in 1935, it was still being used as an open sewer twenty-five years later. Spokane did not have a sewage treatment plant in operation until 1960, long after Pasco, Ellensberg, Walla Walla, and many much smaller communities had working systems.

In the late 1960s a national writer by the name of Neal R. Pierce toured the Western states and wrote an overview called *The Pacific States of America* (1972). Pierce saw Spokane like this:

Physically, Spokane is like warmed-over 1930s except for one very modern parking garage. Two railway lines slice right through the middle of town. The city is terribly ingrown, insular by definition, and has historically been dominated by the most reactionary business groups (especially mining and the railroads). Seattle people hold Spokane in unkind contempt; one told me, 'If you could just move a couple thousand interesting people into Spokane, it would be a pretty fine place to live.' A Seattle economist in 1969 referred to Spokane as a place 'with no real growth elements, even though it has tried to lift itself by its bootstraps with a reasonably successful industrial park.'

One is tempted to say that when you ask Seattlites what Spokane is like you learn mainly what Seattlites are like. In fact, the same writer added to the above passage: "As Seattle slid into deep recession in 1970-1971, Spokane's more diversified agriculture-mining-manufacturing economy continued to hum, raising the question about whom the last laugh might be on." But this ducks a truth even Spokanites were recognizing in the early 1960s. The city had some fundamental problems and was not progressing as it should.

What the cause of this might be was the subject of a great deal of study in the mid-1960s. Dr. Henry Kass, a political scientist at Eastern Washington University who specialized in local government, pointed out in a contemporary study that Spokane was a city of low personal incomes yet high home ownership, meaning it had many "marginal homeowners"—people who had little money to spare after paying the expenses of home ownership and other living expenses. Getting people to tax themselves more for major urban improvements was bound to be an uphill battle, particularly since bond issues required a 60-percent majority to pass.

But even taking this into account, Spokane was an extremely conservative community. Kass compared Spokane with twenty-two other cities about the same size and found that eighteen of them allocated a greater portion of their total incomes to roads, sewers, public buildings and other capital expenditures that upgrade a city. One explanation is that the biggest taxpayers of all were downtown property owners, and in Spokane these property owners had a great deal to say about what the city could or could not afford.

Since the days of Glover and Cannon, Spokane had been a city driven not by political comers, aristocracy, bosses, or absentee millionaires, but by businessmen who worked a full day in their offices and watched events in the city along with all the other variables that might affect business. They owned Spokane—or at least the heart of it, its central business district—and were therefore responsible for it in a way not even the passing political leader could be. They were executives of the major banks and department stores, as well as owners of other downtown buildings, top executives of the Washington Water Power Company, and newspaper publishers. On many matters before the city they had no group interest. But when they did, they could exert powerful influence—as respected opinion leaders, officers in many civic and charitable organizations, as employers of a large portion of the city's population, as lenders, lessors, and in many other ways.

Charles Olmstead, another Eastern Washington University political scientist, writing in the same EWU report as Kass, said: "The size of Spokane, the stability of its population, the close-knit nature of its business and professional world have 'personalized' political and social differences of opinion. The costs of speaking out have often been the heavy ones of personal animosity and sanctions." That no doubt puts too harsh a light on the situation. The city's leadership in these years might be seen as a close-knit, like-minded family which could not understand when someone wanted to rock the boat—and certainly could not allow them to do so. The same group cohesion did a lot of good things. A member of this group could—and often did—pick up the phone and in twenty minutes of calling around town collect any amount of money for a charity or other cause.

The analogy with a close-knit family

The merry-go-round and bumper cars of Natatorium Park continued to thrill Spokane youngsters into the 1950s and 1960s. (EWSHS)

came near to being true because of many intermarriages among Spokane's top families. There were perhaps two dozen key families in Spokane's establishment from approximately 1925 to 1960. By virtue of its longevity and high profile, the Cowles family was in the popular mind the one "that runs Spokane." If not quite equal to that myth, its dual ties to the business community and, through the newspapers, to public opinion, made it immensely influential. Orville C. Pratt, superintendent of Spokane's public schools in the twenties and thirties and an able chronicler of its history, said of the first William Cowles: "In all probability no other citizen of Spokane has had as much influence in determining the sort of city (Spokane) has become. Personally, Cowles was modest, self-effacing, quiet, upright, likeable and inflexible ... It is open to question whether any one man should be in a position to wield such great influence, although with Cowles it was in safe, though conservative hands."

The official history of the *Spokesman-Review, News For An Empire* by Ralph E. Dyar, enumerates the paper's many crusades: for the city's charter change in 1910; against a bonus for World War I veterans; for strong enforcement of Prohibition laws; against local corruption; for many community charities; against rate-setting practices by the railroads that gave coastal cities better rates than Spokane. "A characteristic feature of *The Spokesman-Review's* campaigns in these and other instances," the book says, "was that they were not confined to the columns of the paper. They might include conferences; a war chest; mobilization of public-spirited citizens; speeches before organizations; the appointment of some one person to take charge of a certain campaign; the preparation, printing, and distribution of pamphlets and circulars; the financing of a delegation to go to Washington, D.C., to bring pressure to bear on the lawmakers in the interest of the community; and other missionary work."

That kind of onslaught for the public good was admirable. But what is for the "public good" is not always obvious, and Cowles, as a major property owner downtown, had a built-in conflict of interest. In 1935, the federal government wanted to finance a two million dollar sewage treatment plant for the city under the Works Progress Administration. Because the city would be required to put up the estimated $20,000 a year needed to operate the plant, the project came in for a fierce bombardment on the *Spokesman-Review's* front pages. The first of the articles (December 2, 1935) ran under triple-decked headlines: "Sewage Scheme Causes Alarm ... Plan Voters Rejected Would Mean Big Cost Yearly ... No Health Aid." The story that followed did not quote federal officials about why they were putting the proposal forward, nor the city commissioners about why they might be considering accepting it. Instead, the front page story was a mixture of personal opinion and quotations of others with like opinions:

The WPA's proposed sewage disposal plant gift to the city [the December 2 story began] is one gift horse that is being looked in the mouth by the recipients .... The issue is whether the city has any need for the plant, and if so, whether its value is sufficient that the city should incur a minimum annual charge of $25,000 to keep it working. The state board of health has investigated pollution of the Spokane River, and has found that it is not sufficient to be a nuisance .... Even if there were cities below Spokane, there would be no health menace, because the Spokane River is sufficiently large and swift to carry off the sewage and purify it .... Chief advocates of adding the new sewage disposal tax to

Spokane's expenses are fishermen, who say that if the dumping of sewage into the river stops, there will be good fishing. For $25,000 to $80,000 a year the fishing ought to be extraordinary. . . .

Granted it was another era, one in which publishers felt freer to use their publications for personal advocacy. But this and the other stories in the series were remarkable for totally ignoring every other point of view and even the facts. One would never guess that the state director of health had said two years earlier that Spokane needed a sewage treatment plant "for public health purposes." The state director of health's annual report for that very year, 1935, listed ten rivers in the state in which sewage was a problem. The Spokane River was the first listed and the only one characterized as "grossly polluted" rather than just polluted. The idea that rivers and streams automatically purified themselves, stated as fact in the story, was a popular misapprehension state health authorities were trying to clear up at the time. But no public health authority was quoted in the stories. All the opinions cited were those of Spokane businessmen.

If the voice in the *Spokesman-Review* suggested a curmudgeon, people who knew the senior Cowles found him personally courtly and considerate. He died in 1946 at the age of eighty. Under his son, William, Jr., the *Spokesman-Review* and *Chronicle* became gradually less conservative.

It was not the opposition of the Cowles, nor the parsimony of marginal homeowners, which kept the city from completing so fundamental a public utility as a sewage system for so long—until 1960. *The Spokesman-Review* gave up its opposition in the 1940s and Spokane citizens voted a $1.7 million bond issue to finance a treatment plant in 1946. The state pitched in another one million dollars for the plant—and added an order to the city to quit pouring its sewage into the river. But the city's governing body, the Board of Commissioners, decided in 1948 to reject all the bids for construction of the plant on the grounds that costs of materials may go down later. The five commissioners took the action squabbling, as usual, and there was some suspicion that individual commissioners wanted to use the treatment plant money for more immediate pet projects.

One of the obstacles Spokane had to deal with in the postwar years was its government. In 1910, citizens had adopted the commissioner form of government, which was then considered to offer the ultimate in efficient and responsive urban management. Each elected official would directly manage a group of city departments, so there would never be any question about who was responsible for what. If the roads were bad a citizen could vote against the commissioner of public works; if the police were corrupt the resident could vote against the commissioner of public safety. That was the theory.

In practice, the responsiveness of the commissioners could get out of hand. Since each commissioner made his reputation by redressing complaints against the services he was in charge of delivering, he had no incentive to give up anything in his departments for the larger good. At the same time, a general election is not necessarily the best way to choose a person to oversee the day-to-day details of running a street department or fire department. Instead of responsiveness and efficiency, the commissioner form of government became identified with squabbling and ineptness.

By the mid-1950s, two civic action groups, the Municipal League and the League of Women Voters, had concluded that Spokane should consider changing to the city manager form of government. As the commissioner form of government had been the rage among reformers a half century earlier, now the city manager form, modeled on the management of private corporations, was seen as the way to straighten out city hall. The city manager was a non-political specialist hired to make the city machinery run smoothly and cheaply. He was under the general direction of a kind of "board of directors," a "weak" mayor and council which would set policy but have absolutely no management powers.

Thus, the alternative had already been identified when dissatisfaction with the commissioners finally exploded into revolution. The cause of revolt was the imposition by commissioners of a tax on gross incomes of businesses (a business and occupations, or B&O, tax). With the economy in a slump in the late 1950s, few people liked the idea of a new tax, but to business in particular a B&O tax was anathema. A local advertising man by the name of Charles Devine, always described in the newspapers as representing unnamed "prominent businessmen," announced in November of 1959 that there would be a petition drive aimed at changing the form of government. The Municipal League and the League of Women Voters joined the campaign, and by January of 1960 enough signatures had been gathered to put the matter on a March ballot.

The commissioners responded with a series of actions and statements which at once made them look like men desperately trying to preserve their jobs and made it clear why the government should be changed. Rather than defend the commissioner form, the commissioners suggested that they might put another item on the ballot calling for a change to the *strong* mayor form of government. It was interpreted as an attempt to confuse the issue and led to a series of stormy confrontations between citizens and commissioners. Police and firefighter unions added to the confusion and controversy by collecting money and campaigning to retain the commissioner form of government while at the same time picketing city hall for higher wages. Finally, with the election nearing, four of the commissioners came out of a secret meeting and announced that they had stripped Gaines Sutherlin of the title of mayor (which was bestowed by a vote of the commission) and had named in his place Kenneth Lawson, the one commissioner who had been criticizing just about everything the other commissioners had done for years. Lawson's elevation to mayor could only be interpreted as an admission that things had been about as bad as he had been insinuating all those years.

On March 8, 1960, almost exactly fifty years after adoption of the commissioner form, voters replaced it with a city manager and seven part-time council members. The vote was 30,107 for the change and 19,970 against it.

The following June seven city council members were elected, all but one of them businessmen. The new mayor was Neil R. Fosseen, a vice president of the Old National Bank and the epitome of Spokane's civic/business leaders. Some people had opposed the new form of government on the grounds that it would be less responsive to the general citizenry and more responsive to business—a theory about city manager systems political theorists generally accept. But in the years following the change-over there were no drastic changes in the direction of city services (according to a study by Dr. Kass), except that they became more efficient. In the meantime, Spokane's business community had in effect accepted official responsibility for making the city work. This would be a key to the phenomenal era about to get under way in Spokane.

The years between 1945 and 1960 were

hard-working ones. Dozens of small businesses were started and had to be fanned to life with all the more vigor because of the economic chill. When the people who went to work at Kaiser Aluminum in the late forties began retiring thirty years later, the company suffered a noticeable drop in productivity. Many of those same people were building, evenings and weekends, thousands of new homes added to the city in these years, and most were engaged in rearing the post-war "baby-boom" generation.

The question is, why didn't all this energy translate into civic progress? A city planner by the name of King Cole noticed something about the city when he first arrived in 1963. Its citizens were almost routinely disparaging of it. People referred to the city as "Spokaloo" and "Sin City"—the latter an ironic suggestion that there was nothing to do. The man who installed Cole's telephone said, "You're moving *into* Spokane? I'm getting out as soon as I can." A clerk at the local Payless Store, chatting as she put his purchases in a sack, said, "People are moving out of this city in droves." Charles Olmstead, one of those political scientists scrutinizing Spokane in the mid-sixties, said at the time: "The most pervasive and important attitudinal fact about Spokane is its serious lack of self-awareness . . . The city is unclear as to why it exists, where it is going, and how it will get there."

Thus, as Spokane entered the 1960s, it had a long list of chores to tend to: revive the economy, refurbish the downtown, replace city hall and the airport, and clean up a river still being polluted because the just-opened sewage treatment plant was inadequate. But an even deeper problem was a lack of that pride-in-ownership, that sense of community, which could persuade residents to tend to the city's civic tasks.

Railroad yards, warehouses, and parking lots dominated Havermale and Cannon islands and the Spokane riverfront in this 1966 aerial view. Within the next eight years the area would undergo rapid change, the only remnant of the railroad age being the Great Northern depot tower. (EWSHS)

VII

• SPOKANE RESURGENT ◆

In 1958, Joe Kipper, then president of the Spokane Chamber of Commerce, called an informal meeting of the thirty or so people who owned and managed downtown Spokane. Those gathering in the board room of the original Seattle First National Building at Riverside and Howard included the managers of the department stores, shops and hotels, representatives of all the banks, descendants of mining millionaires Peyton and Paulsen, William Hyde of the Cowles Publishing Company, John Hieber, manager of a large portion of the downtown properties, and Kinsey Robinson of Washington Water Power Company.

What Kipper had to say that day was basically: "If you guys don't wake up you're going to lose your downtown."

To many sitting in the room things did not look so dour. In the last few years, Spokane's downtown had received a new Newberry's store (1952), a new Penney's (1953), an addition to the Crescent (1956), and the Bon Marche store (1957). But Kipper, as manager of the local Sears store, had the perspective of a chain that kept in touch with what was happening nationwide, and what was happening nationwide was that suburban shopping centers were draining the life out of traditional urban centers.

As a result of Kipper's meeting, several of those present formed an organization called Spokane Unlimited to begin planning for the future of the downtown area. The new organization hired a New York urban planning firm called Ebasco Services to draw up a master plan. The so-called "Ebasco Plan," unveiled in 1961, envisioned a huge pedestrian mall replacing automobile traffic on Riverside; six square blocks at the east edge of the central business district devoted to new government buildings and spacious lawns; and a riverfront cleared of railroads and adapted for "cultural uses."

Voters were asked in March of 1962 to launch this ambitious plan by approving a $10.5 million bond issue to build a new city hall and establish the governmental center envisioned in the plan. They said no, and by a huge margin. The results were about the same two years later when a slightly less expensive proposal was put on the ballot. The typical Spokanite did not identify with a "beautified" downtown area. For decades downtown property owners had treated the heart of the city as their own personal business. Now they had made a plan to renovate it without consulting citizens. The voter's attitude was clearly, "pay for it yourself."

Nevertheless, citizens could not just tend to their neighborhoods and ignore what was going on downtown. The city would inevitably be judged by this half-mile-square section, and a vital downtown was Spokane's best chance of improving its entertainment and cultural life. Most of all, the falls was a place of natural beauty which begged to be returned to the whole city. These kinds of considerations spread concern for the city's center beyond the business community. By the mid-1950s "riverfront renewal" was a major topic of conversation at club breakfasts and over private lunches. City Planner Vaughn Call began to hold public hearings in the early sixties on what then seemed impossibly futuristic

Facing page: *Fireworks burst above the United States Pavilion during Expo '74. The U.S. Pavilion theme "Man and Nature: One and Indivisible" was expressed by the quote seen at the pavilion entrance. The words featured on the wall are those of a Northwest Indian chief who rebuked a delegation of white settlers who wanted to buy his land more than a century ago. (EWSHS)*

On June 12, 1972, with less than two years to go until opening day, demolition began on the Expo site. Here a Milwaukee Road crew removes rails east of Union Station, near the present Riverfront Convention Center site. (EWSHS)

plans for a riverfront returned to public use.

To get things moving, the city council tried to get aid through new federal programs which financed urban renewal. But many Spokane citizens were suspicious of strings attached to federal funds, and the debate over seeking federal money consumed much of the energy that went into city politics through the sixties. Those opposed to Spokane's participation in federal programs always won. One more potential avenue toward recovery was blocked.

Spokane Unlimited, too, was groping. In 1963 it hired as its first full-time director King Cole, an affable, articulate attorney-turned-city-planner who had helped San Leandro, California, renovate its downtown and dock area. Many people at Spokane Unlimited were surprised when Cole's first action was to help form a broad-based citizen action group called Associations for a Better Community (ABC). The purpose of the organization, which was made up not of individuals but of representatives of 195 other organizations in the city, was to begin the process of forming a concensus about the community's overall goals.

The following year, 1965, Cole attended a conference in St. Louis, a city which had replaced center-city train tracks and trestles with a park. St. Louis had done it, Cole learned, by getting the National Park Service to stage an exhibition on the site and therefore foot most of the bill for reclaiming the area. Cole returned home and immediately tried to interest the U.S. Park Service in sponsoring some sort of exhibition in Spokane, a city with closer access to more national parks than any other in the country. He got nowhere, but the idea of an exhibition as a catalyst was established.

It was about this time residents began noticing that the city had centennials approaching (whether the proper date to be observed should be 1871, when the first settlers came; 1873, when the first permanent settler came; or 1881, when the city was chartered, was a matter of preference). Cole suggested Spokane Unlimited sieze the opportunity and sponsor an exhibition tied to Spokane's centennial. On his advice Spokane Unlimited hired Economic Research Associates (ERA) of Los Angeles to evaluate the possibility.

The Los Angeles organization reported back that the regional birthday party just wouldn't generate the kind of money needed to produce important changes in the city. Then it made the suggestion that changed Spokane's history. Why not, said the investigators, go all the way and hold a world's fair? The consultants provided a theme, ecology (for this was the emerging concern of the time), and had even taken the liberty of checking with the Bureau of International Exhibitions in Paris and found that there were no conflicting fairs scheduled in the early seventies.

On the basis of ERA's figures and the personal enthusiasm of King Cole, the Spokane Unlimited-sponsored "Spokane Centennial Committee" voted, in late 1970, to change its name to the Expo Corporation. Cole became general manager. The summer of 1974 was chosen because it could be done no earlier, and a later date would clash with celebrations of the nation's bicentennial in 1976.

As simple as that, Spokane had committed itself to producing a world's fair by May 4, 1974. Only gradually, as the requirements of such an undertaking began to take shape over the next couple of years, did people realize what they had gotten themselves into. A world's fair is a colossal undertaking, even for a larger city with lots of capital to draw on. Spokane had the minimum amount of time to put a fair together—and could not even start until it dealt with the sticky problem of moving three railroads. And the Spokane River was still quite polluted because of Spokane's inadequate sewage treatment plant and dozens of polluters upstream as far as the mines of Idaho. Did Spokane dare invite the world to come to talk about ecology on a site that overlooked a polluted river? Two of the city's oldest and most formidable problems—reclaiming the river from the railroads and cleaning up the river water—had become mere prerequisites to a larger project.

Long afterwards, many of those who had created Expo would admit that if they had had any idea of what the effort would require, they might not have taken it on. But by the time that dawned, it was too late to back out gracefully. The only exit was straight ahead through forty months that would change the city as much as it had changed in forty years.

The thing that pulled it through was a singularity of purpose and cohesion few cities could muster. World's fairs, which involve lots of money, lots of people and drastic changes in the city's life, are typically riven with disputes. In Spokane the odds were long enough and the stakes large enough that the city went on a kind of emergency footing. Differences were laid aside. The deadline ruled out equivocation and delay. Every resource and every person in the city was subject to being drafted to the cause.

The Expo board of directors included forty-eight opinion leaders from all phases of life in the community. The executive committee that would take care of the day-to-day decisions was made up of twelve people who represented most of the city's financial resources: Roderick Lindsay of Lincoln First Federal Savings and Loan Association; James P. Brennan of First National Bank; James G. Critzer of Critzer Equipment Company; James P. Cowles of Cowles Publishing Company; Vern W. Johnson of Vern W. Johnson and Sons, Inc., general contractors; E.A. Coon of Seattle-First National Bank; Kinsey M. Robinson of Washington Water Power Company; Philip H. Stanton of Washington Trust Bank; Edwin J. McWilliams of Fidelity Mutual Savings Bank; Bruce H. McPhaden of Kaiser Aluminum Company; Lawrence V. Brown of Pack River Company; and Joseph J. Rosenfield of SRO Favorite Theaters, Inc. Significantly, nearly all those on the executive committee were the chief executives in their own banks and companies. When money was needed, these people wouldn't have to go back and make a presentation to a budget committee. The committee was headed up by Roderick A. Lindsay, a powerful personality who had taken over his father's bank in the depths of the Depression and built it into the multi-million-dollar Lincoln Savings and Loan Association.

But even Lindsay and his band of chief executive officers did not have the wherewithal to put on a world's fair by themselves. The plan was that the city, with its access to tax revenues and government aid, would acquire ownership of the land along the river and build a park on it. This park, however, would be loaned as the site of a six-month exposition—which would leave in its wake a civic center and all sorts of other residuals the city could afford no other way.

The plan almost floundered from the start because a city bond issue, which was to provide $5.7 million to create a park on the river, failed to get the necessary 60 percent approval (though it did get a healthy majority, 56 percent). The only option left to the city to raise the money was the dreaded business and occupations tax, the very one that had caused a revolt against city government a decade earlier. Mayor David H. Rodgers (who succeeded Neil Fosseen in 1967) called a mass meeting of the city's organizations, ranging from the Chamber of Commerce to the League of Women Voters and National Association for the Advancement of Colored People. He asked for and received a concensus that the council should raise the money by imposing a new business and occupations tax. On the night the city council voted to impose the new tax, only one person stood up to protest. Spokane had begun to unite behind a purpose.

One reason such a small city could put on a fair of this size was that the whole of city government became virtually a part of the Expo staff. Mayor Rodgers had a solid four votes on the council to approve anything necessary to make Expo work. Sometimes, to keep up with relentless Expo deadlines, city staff members took actions on the career-risking trust that the council would back them up retroactively.

City Manager F. Sylvin Fulwiler had assigned the city's chief engineer, Glen A. Yake, to head up city government's part of the effort. Robust, popular, often controversial, Yake had shepherded hundreds of engineering projects from design to approval in his thirty years with the city, and no one was in a better position to coordinate all the machinery of local government and dozens of private contractors.

Yake's first job was to secure for the city ownership of the riverfront property. There were thirty owners of land to be dealt with one by one, but the important three were the railroads. The Union Pacific alone had once estimated that its properties on the riverfront were worth

As soon as the riverfront railroad tracks were dismantled, the wrecking ball went to work on the Great Northern depot. On February 5, 1973, the clock tower warned that only 450 days remained until the World's Fair would begin. The tower itself was left in the park as a reminder of the role railroads played in Spokane's development. (EWSHS)

about $16 million. The Expo board and the city replied at an early meeting that they would like to see the railroads simply donate the land. This idea was the cause of open merriment among railroad officials at one of the initial meetings. But Yake and King Cole kept after the railroads with an argument that finally proved persuasive (and, as it turned out, true). The railroads, they argued, could donate the primary land, but hold on to fringe property. The new park would increase the value of these surrounding parcels of land so much the railroads would profit in the long run.

The railroads finally capitulated, donating all of the riverfront property. But they said they would sign only when the city had straightened out legal complications. What seemed like a reasonable stipulation in fact became one of the major obstacles to producing Expo. In nearly a century of operations through Spokane, the three railroads had built up a tangled mass of trades, agreements, and legal technicalities which encumbered every piece of property. Yake and the city's legal staff had to straighten out these encumbrances to get clear title, and couldn't do so without railroad cooperation. But railroad officials, sitting in their offices in Chicago or Milwaukee, far from the pressing deadlines of Spokane's exposition, appeared to give the situation a low priority. When Yake would try to contact them with an urgent problem, sometimes his call was returned and sometimes it wasn't.

When it wasn't, he called Jim Cowles, the younger grandson of the founder of

Spokane's newspapers. James and his brother, William Cowles, III, had taken over the family business in the late 1960s, including management of two and one-half blocks of very valuable downtown property. Though they were wont to caution others against putting a Cowles out front in the Expo effort—it might stir up the old questions about the family running Spokane—the two brothers played a key role in the fifteen-year effort to upgrade the city's center.

James Cowles is invariably listed as one of the people most important to making Expo a success. He got involved in many aspects of the fair, but his specific assignment from the Expo board of directors was to deal with the railroads. His influence with them was not entirely clear to anyone. Apparently the Cowles Publishing Company took its considerable banking business to a bank with strong ties to the Union Pacific. Also, the Cowles-owned Inland Paper Company was a major shipper with railroads. But Cowles' effectiveness with the sluggish railroad bureaucracies appeared to be based upon dogged persistence as much as anything. At one point he had architect Tom Adkison work through a weekend, redrawing the Expo plans to show a world's fair taking place on a site still containing remnants of the railroads. Cowles took the plans to Milwaukee to show railroad officials *they* were going to be the ones embarrassed if things didn't start to happen on the site. When John Kenefick, the president of Union Pacific Railroad, came to Spokane for a pre-Expo function, he leaned over to Mayor Rodgers and said, "Would you mind pointing out this fellow Jim Cowles to me?" "I got the impression," Rodgers said later, "that he had had some pretty

City manager F. Sylvin Fulwiler (left) and chief engineer Glen A. Yake hammer out details of city's acquisition of riverfront land.

firm conversations with Jim."

A remarkable thing about Spokane's Expo effort is that it had many obstacles, but each time there seemed to be someone especially equipped to lift it over the hurdles. If the railroads were going to give up their stations on the riverfront, they would have to agree to share facilities in the Northern Pacific station at the south edge of the city's business district. Approval of such consolidations by the U.S. Interstate Commerce Commission often took months. In Spokane's case it took seven days. The reason was that the chairman of the U.S. Senate committee that oversees ICC business was Senator Warren G. Magnuson of Washington State. Senator Magnuson, one of the Senate's most powerful legislators, arranged for a long list of federal subsidies to Expo, only one example of which was the $11.5 million Federal Pavilion "tent."

The Expo plan drawn up by Economic Research Associates had as one of its essential requirements the construction of a $7.5 million convention hall and auditorium. This was both necessary for the Exposition and was one of the main prizes the city expected to get for all this effort. This, people in Spokane thought, would be the ideal contribution of the State of Washington.

Getting the state to go along, however, was going to be difficult because the legislature was both controlled by interests on the west side of the state and in a conservative mood.

To deal with the legislature the Expo board called in Luke Williams, Jr. Luke and his brother Chuck had invented in their garage in the Spokane Valley what was to become a part of the American scene: the lighted-up sign panel capable of flashing ever-changing messages and pictures. Their Spokane-based company, American Sign & Indicator, built signs for customers around the world, from New York City's Times Square to Saudi Arabia, and in the process Luke had become both wealthy and well-known in business circles. And, he was active in Chamber of Commerce and conservative Republican circles. Expo chairman Roderick Lindsay, a former Democratic state legislator himself, could deal with Democrats in the legislature. It was the Republicans who might be a problem, so Williams, reminded of his civic duties and apprised of the situation, was sent off in his private airplane to talk to business and Republican friends around the state. The legislature provided the $7.5 million original appropriation and later supplemented that with another three million dollars.

When even that second appropriation ran short—for the plans for the Opera House became more ambitious as time went on—Williams recruited Vickie McNeill, an experienced local fundraiser for charities, to contact donors all over the city and state to raise another one million dollars for finishing touches.

This is how Expo would be built: with volunteer work and mostly outside money. The cost of preparing the fair site alone would be a minimum of sixty million dollars, and that kind of money did not exist in Spokane. Spokane businesses had pooled six million dollars in "seed" money to get the effort organized, and besides had taxed themselves to spruce up the downtown area with trees, new benches, and new street lamps. The rest of the money was picked up bit by bit. When there was no money to buy out a thriving motel occupying part of the prospective fair site, Mayor Rodgers called the Comstock Foundation, a local philanthropic group. It bought the land and gave it to the city. When there had to be a new bridge passing through the site at Washington Street, City Councilman Del Jones and Glen Yake persuaded the state's Urban Arterial Board to declare the situation an emergency and put up the funds. When money for putting finishing touches on the site ran low, City Councilman Jack O'Brien suggested the ultimately successful stratagem of applying for a grant from the U.S. Economic Development Agency on the grounds that a successful Expo would boost Spokane's economy.

If preparing a site for the fair was a scramble, bringing exhibitors to it was even more so. Lee Iaccoca, then president of the Ford Motor Company, said his first response when it was suggested that Ford become an exhibitor in Spokane was, "Where the hell's Spokane?" That was the essence of the problem for Expo recruiters. Many doubted five million people would go so far out of the way to visit the fair, and so potential exhibitors were tempted to say no without even looking the proposition over. King Cole's strategy was to have Spokanites with national contacts get a representative to at least come out and take a look. Once here, the national representative was entertained in private homes, chauffered around, introduced to friendly contractors and union leaders who guaranteed there would be no labor disputes to contend with. Spokane, it seemed, could arrange just about anything for an exhibitor. In the fall of 1972, Walt Toly, the recently retired president of Columbia Heating and Light and now head of the effort to entice American exhibitors to Expo, brought top executives from General Motors, Ford, Kodak, IBM, and other companies to Spokane for a sales pitch. He tramped them across the site and then took them to the YMCA building on Havermale Island and showed them slides of what the fair would look like. There was just one problem. The feature attraction, the river, was almost bone dry. Toly explained that during most of the Fair this rock canyon would be boiling with snowmelt. Then he said, "Look, I'll show you." Several miles up the river Kinsey Robinson, president of the Washington Water Power Company, had personally ordered the dams opened, and at noon, as scheduled, a wall of water smashed through the basalt canyon even as the executives watched. They were impressed.

Expo's breakthrough with international exhibitors came in the wake of a breakthrough in international politics. The very day President Richard Nixon was in Moscow signing agreements which were part of the general warming of U.S.—USSR relations known as "detente," King Cole was sitting in the George V Hotel bar with Boris Borisov, chairman of the Soviet Chamber of Commerce and Industry. In the spirit of detente the Soviets committed to an immense exhibit that would cover a full acre and was four times as large as the Soviet exhibit at the 1962 Seattle World's Fair. This early, large-scale participation by the Soviet Union did more than anything else to legitimize Expo '74 as an international exhibit.

The first foreign exhibitor to sign on was, naturally enough, Canada. It agreed to occupy the key island which now bears its name. But that agreement precipitated a major crisis in Expo's development. One year before the opening of Expo the national Canadian government in Ottawa decided almost routinely to reduce a budget deficit by eliminating the funds which had been set aside for the Spokane exhibit. News of this caused near panic in Spokane. Other exhibitors then being courted—indeed, perhaps the others that had already committed—might wonder if this really was a "world's fair" if even this close neighbor would not participate.

Luckily, Western Canadians reacted swiftly and angrily to their national government's decision. Editorials in Canadian newspapers blasted the decision while bumper stickers appeared on Canadian cars that read, "To Hell With Ottawa,

We're Going To Spokane." The protests caused the national Canadian government to reverse its decision. It is entirely possible that long-time friends to the north saved Spokane's world's fair.

The very audacity of the whole Expo project had guaranteed there would be constant crises like this, which piled pressure on top of heavy work loads. Everyone knew, Expo Executive Vice President David Peterson would say later, that they were either involved in one of the great experiments of urban revitalization, or an ignominious flop that would be recounted by the press all over the world: "People said, 'You can't do it, you can't do it.' Then we had the state involved, then the federal government. Then we were in *Time* magazine and everybody in the nation was watching us. You feel that tension when you go home at night. If we didn't make it, Spokane was going to be 'The Little City That Couldn't.'"

The U.S. Department of Commerce was among those getting nervous. It had both money and prestige invested in the Spokane Fair, and it didn't want to see a flop. It was accustomed to watching world's fairs develop, furthermore, and no doubt it had never seen a fair built like this—by people who went about begging every board as it was needed.

Early in the summer before Expo, Department of Commerce officials called Rod Lindsay to Washington, D.C., and flatly threatened to ask Congress to withdraw its support for the fair if changes were not made in its management. Whether department officials would or could make good on such a threat was another question. But any open debate about the fair at this point, when the city was beginning its publicity campaign to get visitors to come, would have been disastrous. Besides, Lindsay and other members of the executive board did not necessarily disagree that a shake-up would be healthy. Lindsay decided on his own to take the department's advice. He interviewed three professional fair managers and hired Petr Spurney as general manager.

Expo president King F. Cole (left) and J. Welles Henderson, U.S. commissioner general for Expo '74, survey construction at the Expo site.

Many of the executive board were livid when Lindsay returned to Spokane and told them what he had done. There was a fierce proprietary feeling about Expo by this time, and board members resented the federal agency's meddling. The "sense of command" so many admired in Lindsay now began to look like sheer arbitrariness. Around the board table there were loud voices, flushed faces, angry tapping of pencils. For the first time the unity which had brought the city this far was threatened. But Lindsay reminded them that there was no turning back at this point, and the crisis passed.

Many of those who had worked on Expo for three years before Petr Spurney arrived felt Spurney gave the impression that he had personally made it a success, and they resented it. But most would concede that Spurney contributed to the fair by providing specialized knowledge of concessionaires, organizing advertising and publicity, and scheduling on-site entertainment.

Spokane's distinction in the history of world's fairs is that it was the first to so thoroughly subordinate the short-term celebration to the long-term benefits. Such facilities as the Opera House, housing for the Carousel (which served as a "Bavarian Beer Garden" for the duration of the fair) and Boeing Amphitheater were all planned not for a fair but for the future.

The fair's general architect, Tom Adkison, was a long-time member of the Spokane Park Board. Always, as he laid out the park for Expo, he kept in mind the park that would follow it. He conceptualized a park of contrasts. Isolated pathways would open suddenly onto broad fields. The sense of an untamed, unmanageable river in the north channels would be heightened by suspended bridges which swung over the water, as if it were too wild to touch. The south channel Forebay, by contrast, would be highly structured and sculpturesque, with steps descending right into the water and bridges with legs firmly sunk in the slow-moving water.

City and country would mix in the park. Hollows and hills suggest rural beauty, while the Great Northern Clock Tower, the Carousel, and the Parsian beauty of the Washington Street Bridge would represent the best in urban forms. The new was blended with the old when lamp poles which had stood on Spokane downtown streets since the 1920s were shortened, fitted with new glass and used to light the park's pathways.

These plans were translated into a fair by dozens of contractors under the direction of general contractor Vern Johnson of Spokane. Until late in the spring of 1974 the view through the chain link fences that surrounded the site was one of mud, materials, and machinery in motion. Because much of the grass was saved to be laid down at the last minute, people who looked at the site from the outside wondered if it could possibly be shaped up by opening day. In fact it was finished a day early.

It was very cool the morning of May 4, 1974, 38 degrees at 6:00 a.m. But as the sun rose in a clear blue sky the air warmed and took on the sweet vibrancy typical of Spokane mornings in early spring or late fall. Twenty thousand people crowded around the north side of the new Opera House to observe opening day ceremonies. Expo officials, representatives of the nine foreign nations exhibiting at the fair, and local political representatives, gathered on a stage floating in the Forebay. President Nixon (who had just a few days earlier released the "Watergate tapes" which would lead to his resignation only four months later) arrived shortly before noon to declare Expo '74 "open to the world."

Eighty-five thousand went through the gates on opening day. The millionth visitor showed up June 8, and by the time the six-month fair was over, 5.6 million had purchased tickets, pushing attendance over projections by a million.

Fair-goers could visit nine national exhibits (from Australia, Canada, the Federal Republic of Germany, Iran, Japan, the Republic of China, the Republic of Korea, the Phillipines, the Soviet Union, and the United States; seven exhibits by Northwest states and Canadian provinces; sixty-two industrial exhibits (including General Motors, Ford Motor Company, Kodak, and Kaiser Aluminum); and twenty-six "special category" exhibits (ranging from the Afro-American exhibit to that of the Washington State Wheat Commission). Four open-air stages, including one floating in the Forebay behind the Opera House, were booked through the day and evening with entertainment from all over the world. A central food fair and a dozen specialty restaurants, brass bands, mimes, jugglers, and magicians, plus a daily average of 30,000 people swarming the pathways, added up to an experience hard to imagine now on the peaceful grounds of Riverfront Park.

One of the two most popular exhibits was the Soviet Pavilion, where an unsmiling bronze Vladimir Lenin welcomed visitors into an acre of dioramas, scientific displays, and a lime-colored fantasy representing the biosphere. The other crowd-pleaser was under the tent of the U.S. Pavilion, where giant insects dangling overhead carefully arranging heaps of junk mocked the human propensity toward spoiling their own nest. In the IMAX Theater an audience listening to an Indian the size of a four-story building talk about the environment suddenly found their chairs seemingly falling out from under them as they "flew" through the narrows of the Grand Canyon, skimming above the river. The Korean exhibit featured "The Sounds of Nature"—recorded sounds of birds, voices, and moving water—while the Iranian exhibit displayed ancient Persian artifacts. Japan constructed a Japanese Garden at the entrance to a theater where costumed women performed traditional dances. From the belting cheeriness of the "Up With People" singers in the General Motors Pavilion one could descend into the cave-like darkness of a section of the Australian Pavilion and look a rare reptile or an inverted bat in the eye. An art exhibit in the new Convention Center displayed the works of Audubon, Remington, Russell, Wyeth, Grandma Moses, Mark Tobey, and other American masters; a short walk beyond that was the gaudy Midway. And at every turn there was the rediscovered river itself. A record runoff that May and June sent a canyon full of water tumbling over itself and foaming white in its rush to the Falls.

Spokane's past was showcased at Expo's Folklife Festival. Visitors could enjoy the daily logging exhibitions and the authentic Indian dances or watch their names stitched into a huge quilt. In one of the most popular exhibits fairgoers could pan gold brought in from an Idaho claim. (EWSHS)

What a strange sight it was for a Spokanite of that era, strolling along the river on a fragrant summer evening, to look across the reflecting waters of the Forebay to a renewed cityscape and see the Opera House lit up with a famous name on the marquee—Jack Benny; John Denver; Bob Hope; Van Cliburn; Victor Borge; Jose Feliciano; the Philadelphia or Los Angeles Philharmonics; the Joffrey Ballet; the Leningrad Ballet.

During the six months of the fair, a series of symposia held in nearby buildings explored the large questions that a world

Facing page: *The Spokane Ad Club held a contest in 1911 to come up with a design for its stationery letterhead. The winning entry introduced "Miss Spokane"—an Indian princess wearing a symbol of the sun to honor the Spokane tribe which called itself "Children of the Sun." She held a sheaf of wheat in one hand in reference to the area's agricultural wealth, and a jug of pouring water to represent the abundance of water in the region. In 1912, Margarite Motie was selected to add life to the letterhead, and to be the city's first official hostess. She continued to serve as Miss Spokane until 1939. This glass window was made from the original design by John A. Scott who presented it to the Chamber of Commerce in 1972. (EWSHS)*

exposition on the environment had raised. Authorities from around the world came to Spokane to discuss the pollution of the oceans, air, soil and the exhaustion of natural resources—dangers which, strange as it would seem later, had hardly begun to penetrate world consciousness.

Expo itself was a practical statement on such problems. It was publicized across the country and was studied by many other cities as a model of what a community could do if it perceived a problem, found a plan, and worked together. Almost unnoticed in the excitement of the fair was the fact that Spokane had built (mostly with federal funds) a sewage treatment plant which cost more than the Federal Pavilion, the Opera House, and all the landscaping of Riverfront Park combined. This project, which was under way before Expo, had been supplemented by a massive, Expo-inspired study of the entire Spokane River basin. The study helped cease the flushing of pollutants into the Spokane River by mines, lumber mills, plants, and towns between Idaho and the Columbia River. Within a few years these efforts brought the river closer to its natural purity than it had been in this century.

Expo had begun to have its intended effect on the downtown long before opening day. The JC Penney Company, impressed by Spokane's revival, reversed a company policy of rebuilding only in shopping centers and established a new store in Spokane's downtown. Its old building was remodeled and occupied by Nordstrom. The skywalk system, a remnant of the Ebasco Plan, began in the early seventies to link all buildings downtown, creating a second downtown one story above the first, a unique idea that gained national publicity. A new hotel on the riverfront (the Sheraton), two new bank towers (Sea-First and Washington Trust), the new Cowles-built parking garage, and such notable restorations as the 1889 Building and the Bennett Block added to what would be one of the most successful examples of urban revival in the country.

At the center of this revival, as planned, was the new Riverfront Park. When it opened in 1976 people swarmed to it—settling all doubts about whether a city-center park could attract people.

The single most popular aspect of the new park turned out to be the seventy-year-old Carousel from Natatorium Park. Purchased years earlier through a city-wide fund drive, it immediately began contributing $50,000 per year to the park's upkeep.

The Carousel is a symbol of continuity in Spokane. Children who ride the Carousel today could be the great-great-grandchildren of those who rode it when it came to Spokane in 1911.

The Carousel stands at the corner of Howard and Spokane Falls Boulevard—right back where this story began. Jimmy Glover himself ordained the location and dimensions of this, Spokane's first, intersection. Fifty feet to the east, a grassy spot just above the Forebay now, is where James Nosler, the hardworking but tragic pioneer had his first land office in Spokane Falls. Diagonally across the boulevard is the corner where the irrepressible Anthony Cannon had his store and bank. Directly across the street is the Coeur d'Alene Hotel, Dutch Jake's building, the very heap of bricks which once vibrated with piano music and the desperate laughter of the miners and maidens of Spokane's turn-of-the-century honkey-tonk district.

What stories this little spot of earth has seen.

And will see yet. For we come to the end of a book only. Tomorrow morning the streets of Spokane will be lit by the first low beams of sunlight, and the story goes on.

SPOKANE

Trees and shrubs from around the world flourish alongside native species in Finch Memorial Arboretum, on the Sunset Hill. The city park board used a donation from the estate of Spokane mining capitalist John A. Finch to purchase the forty-five acres for the arboretum. Courtesy, Richard Heinzen

Above: *Cannon Hill Park, near the crest of the south hill, is one of sixty parks in the city. Courtesy, Richard Heinzen*

Right: *The Spokane-Nishinomiya Japanese Tea Garden, in Manito Park, is considered one of the most authentic in the U.S. Courtesy, Richard Heinzen*

Facing page: *This 1981 view of an old barn in the wheatfields of the Spokane Valley looks as though it could have been taken a century ago. Courtesy, Earl Roberge*

Right: *The first snow delicately transforms the Spokane landscape. Courtesy, Richard Heinzen*

Right: *These unusual rock formations, known familiarly as the "Bowl and Pitcher," have attracted thousands of visitors to Riverside State Park, three miles northwest of the city. The rocks are remnants of a one-mile-thick basaltic shelf that once blanketed the Inland Empire. Land for Riverside State Park was secured by Aubrey L. White, the founding president of the Spokane Park Board. The suspension bridge near the "Bowl and Pitcher" was built by the Civilian Conservation Corps, and opened in May of 1941. Courtesy, Richard MacLeod*

Above: *Only thirty miles northeast of the city, Mt. Spokane attracts skiers, snowmobilers, and other Inland Empire winter sports enthusiasts. Mt. Spokane State Park is one of four major ski resorts within ninety minutes of Spokane. Courtesy, Richard Heinzen*

Left: *Spokane pioneer James Monaghan had this home built for his wife, who died shortly before its completion in 1895. The Monaghan home, at East 217 Boone Avenue, has been used as a music conservatory by Gonzaga University since 1939. Courtesy, Richard Heinzen (EWSHS)*

Left: *The dramatic Spokane Opera House graces Riverfront Park in this 1985 view. Courtesy, Richard Heinzen*

Facing page: *Spokane Indian teepees once stood where professional and amateur golfers now tee off at Indian Canyon Golf Course. The municipal course, west of Spokane, is one of nine public eighteen-hole courses in and around the city. Courtesy, Richard Heinzen*

Left: *Downtown Spokane had regained its vitality in this 1980 view of the Parkade Plaza. Courtesy, Earl Roberge*

Left: *This 1976 aerial shows the expanse of Spokane from the falls to the mountains. Courtesy, Earl Roberge*

Left: *Rising more than 270 feet from the street, the Sea-First Financial Center was by far the tallest Spokane skyscraper when it opened in May of 1982. The twenty-story tower provided 160,000 square feet of new office space and joined half a dozen other large structures added to the city skyline within the previous decade. Courtesy, Richard Heinzen*

Since German immigrant Frederick Post built his first sawmill, the Spokane River has provided the power to process building materials for homes and industries throughout the Northwest. It is estimated that one-fourth of the nation's stand of soft timber is located in the Inland Empire. Courtesy, Richard Heinzen

Left: *Crowds of Spokanites meet and relax at Riverfront Park, where the Great Northern Railroad once had its railyard. Courtesy, Richard Heinzen*

Above: *The immense USSR exhibit was one of the top attractions at Expo '74. (EWSHS)*

Left: *A bike rider zips by the opera house along Riverfront Park. Courtesy, Richard Heinzen*

Above: *The gently rolling hills of the Palouse country sweep to the horizon in this 1983 view. Courtesy, Earl Roberge*

Right: *The historic Spokane Flour Mill has a new life as a multi-level shopping mall. The Flour Mill began to tie the north side of the river to the life of downtown. Courtesy, Richard Heinzen*

Left: *The clock tower and U.S. Pavilion frame this view of Riverfront Park on a sunny September afternoon in 1976. Courtesy, Richard Heinzen*

Below: *Spokanites take time to enjoy a romantic stroll in the park. Courtesy, Richard Heinzen*

WASHINGTON WATER

Facing page: *The gondola ride across the Spokane River continues to give Spokanites and visitors a thrilling view of the falls. Courtesy, Richard Heinzen*

This May 1974 overview of Expo shows it in full swing.

Above: *Dancers from China prepare to perform at Expo '74.*

Right: *A bust of Lenin greeted visitors to the USSR pavilion, the largest foreign exhibit at Expo.*

Far left: *The Spokane River forebay lights up at night as Expo visitors get a dramatic view of the sprawling fairgrounds.*

Left: *Jeanne Lewis, a nine-year-old from Toppenish, Washington, gets ready for a dance contest.*

Below: *USSR National Day featured a performance by the Moiseyev Dance Company.*

SPOKANE HARDWARE CO
19

• Partners In Progress •

Facing page: *Thomas F. Conlan and A.P. Wolverton organized the Spokane Hardware Company in January of 1886. Conlan, standing with his back to the camera, bought out Wolverton in 1888 and remained with the company until 1910. In 1892, a year before this photo, Conlan built this two-story building to house his store on Riverside Avenue, west of the Sherwood Building. (EWSHS)*

The history of business is an important aspect of Spokane's past. Commerce and industry helped make Spokane a city and the economic center of a vast intermountain hinterland.

In every large community new businesses are formed almost daily. Only a few survive, and they acquire economic strength that affects not only the lives and well-being of owners, employees, and customers, but also of the city as a whole. If business is not the heart, the soul, or the mind of the community, it is at least its lifeblood.

Three moments in Spokane's history seem to have been especially propitious for business formation. Early opportunities arose during Spokane's growth years, particularly in the decade after the fire when new construction and a surging population transformed a frontier settlement into an important Western city. During this period Spokane became an established financial, transportation, and distribution center.

After World War I Spokane's period of rapid growth was replaced by a more tempered pace of business activity and then, in concert with the nation, economic depression. World War II and New Deal spending helped to reverse the decline, and Spokane entered a second phase of significant growth and new business formation in the decade following 1945.

The plateau that was reached in the sixties provided a solid foundation for a revival of business activity in the seventies. Shaken from complacency, Spokane's business leaders embraced an enthusiasm that was reflected both in Expo '74 and in the spate of high-tech business starts that link Spokane industry to the future.

What transformations the future will bring are difficult to predict. Major changes in Spokane-area business and industry have already occurred, such as a diminished role for Northwest forest products and farms that can produce food in abundance but only wafer-thin margins of profit. Other natural-resource industries, such as mining and electric power generation, remain important—but no longer demand the legions of employees that made Spokane a destination for job-hungry workers in years past.

The changes of tomorrow are occurring now, gradually and often silently. Spokane, once proud to be the hub of the Inland Empire, increasingly looks beyond its backyard to the marketplace of the world.

Today businesses of all kinds flourish in Spokane. Some are industry leaders in advanced-technology fields. Others perform more traditional tasks in banking, retailing, and manufacturing. Still others provide services, such as education, medical care, and communication.

Many are the businesses that have helped to shape Spokane. Those whose stories appear on the following pages have chosen to support the publication of this book. In this way they have contributed to making the history of Spokane—including that of its businesses—a resource for the future.

SPOKANE HISTORIC PRESERVATION FOUNDATION

Riverside Avenue in the 1920s, showing (from left to right) the Empire State Building, Cascade Block, Crescent Building, and Review Building. Courtesy, Eastern Washington State Historical Society

Established in 1983, the Spokane Historic Preservation Foundation has a short past but a large vision. Its mission is to assist Spokane's city and county residents to preserve their historic heritage through close cooperation with the City/County Historic Landmarks Commission, primarily by providing financial assistance to owners of properties that are listed on the Spokane Register of Historic Places.

The historic preservation movement is relatively new to Spokane, a city that only recently began the process of renewing the architectural stock contributed by successive generations of founders and builders. This growth by accretion was a passive form of preservation. Then came Expo and the active desire to give Spokane a modern and progressive image. The city center sprouted the bright glass and steel facades of contemporary architecture, but in the process some landmark buildings were lost to the wrecking ball.

The transformation of the cityscape during the 1970s spurred to action individuals concerned about historic preservation. In 1978, through the efforts of the Junior League of Spokane, an inventory of Spokane's historic resources was adopted by the City Plan Commission, and the Spokane City/County Historic Landmarks Commission was established.

By 1981 the commission had drawn up a preservation ordinance that was then adopted by both city and county government. In the same year the city passed a historic preservation plan. These local provisions complement federal and state historic preservation statutes that resulted from President Lyndon Johnson's "Great Society" legislation passed in 1966.

The federal Historic Preservation Act established funding and a regulatory context for state and local efforts. This legislation, implemented by the National Park Service, Department of the Interior, eventually led to the inclusion of thirty-seven Spokane County properties on the National Register of Historic Places.

In Spokane, primary responsibility for coordination of historic preservation activities rests with a full-time historic preservation officer. The preservation officer organizes workshops on historic preservation, disseminates information concerning various incentives for rehabilitation, prepares educational materials for public use, and reviews projects for their impact on historic properties.

The agenda for Spokane's historic-preservationist community is ambitious. It seeks not only to save individual buildings of architectural and historic value, but also to preserve the integrity of representative sections of the city. This has been done by establishing Historic Districts, such as the segment of Riverside Avenue between Monroe and Walnut streets, and Peaceful Valley, which is representative of a working-class neighborhood of turn-of-the-century Spokane.

Compared to the history of mankind, of western civilization, or even of the United States, the history of Spokane appears as a fleeting moment. Yet many Spokanites already feel the need to preserve tangible reminders of the city's collective past. The earlier generations of Spokane County inhabitants, in the words of historic preservation officer Janice Rutherford, "have left behind a special heritage in the structures they built—a heritage that is our privilege to enjoy and conserve."

The James N. Glover House, built by K.K. Cutter in 1889. Glover was known as the "Father of Spokane." Courtesy, Eastern Washington State Historical Society

QUALITY INN SPOKANE HOUSE

In the early nineteenth century Northwest Company traders and trappers operated their Spokane House near the confluence of the Spokane and Little Spokane rivers. It stood out as a source of hospitality for explorers traveling through Indian lands. A century and a half later, a modern hostelry revived the name for its motor inn and restaurant perched above the city on Sunset Boulevard.

The name was a later inspiration. When it opened in 1952 the Spokane House was known as the Desert Caravan Inn—named after its original Desert family owners. But by the late 1950s the inn had acquired its current name and a national ranking, especially for its restaurant.

Today the Spokane House again enjoys a reputation for quality under the management of Terry Wynia, who, with his wife, Jean, and sister, Lynda Greene, bought the establishment in 1978. Prior to their purchase the inn had lost some of its former luster, when, following the death of its founder in the early 1970s, the property was operated by the Spokane subsidiary of a Canadian oil firm.

This "turn-around" situation was made to order for Wynia. He did much of his growing up in Spokane, where his father was a retail grocer. Then the elder Wynia moved his family to the Tri-Cities area where he operated a motel. There Terry got a head start on his education in the hostelry business.

By the time he finished, Wynia had to his credit a master's degree in hotel and restaurant management, several years' experience working for most of the major national hotel and motel groups, and a stint as a faculty member at the University of Nevada-Las Vegas. He was then ready for a homecoming and a challenge.

The Spokane House provided the opportunity he sought. It had suffered from neglect, and no longer offered customers the same value as before. Wynia's management expertise reversed the decline. Within two years the occupancy rate had doubled, from 30 to 60 percent, and it has since climbed to a healthy 80 percent.

The key? Boosting the morale of employees and encouraging them to excel at their jobs, restoration of the lost luster, and satisfied customers who supply word-of-mouth advertising.

Wynia believes that his new Quality Inn North, which opened in May 1984, will also fill a need for quality accommodations at moderate prices. As at the Spokane House and the Quality Inn Valley, which he manages as well, Wynia advocates "an old-time innkeeping attitude," like that which made Spokane a safe haven for Northwest Company traders and trappers.

A panoramic view of Spokane and the Bitterroot Mountains from the Quality Inn Spokane House.

APPLEWAY CHEVROLET

John Pring (left) stands behind one of his two showroom models at the original Appleway Chevrolet location on Appleway (Sprague Avenue) at Argonne Road.

Although he is apt to call himself a gambler, it is probably more accurate to say that from his early childhood John Pring developed the art of taking calculated risks. He still remembers vividly the mental sifting and weighing that accompanied his decision, at age six, to buy his first horse. He had come to an auction in Lewiston, Idaho, and found a beautiful mount. The auctioneer urged him to bid, assuring him that his father would approve. No sooner had young John opened the bidding than the auctioneer declared it closed. Before long, John's father was committed not only to buying the horse, but also to equipping it with bridle and saddle. John remembers wondering whether his father "would skin him alive"—but he bet on the people and the trust he placed in them, and won.

By age eight John Pring had discovered an entrepreneurial spirit as well. With some other Lewiston boys as partners, John operated an ash-hauling service for residential customers, using the neighboring Catholic priest's black buggy for drayage.

In 1921 the Pring family moved from Lewiston to Dishman, where John's father became a highly successful life insurance agent. John Pring learned a lot about salesmanship from his father, but resisted the invitation to follow in his footsteps. He wanted to strike out on his own. He first found work in California desert gold mines. But three years of this was enough, and in 1925 he returned home to invest his $5,000 savings.

As his first venture he staged a rodeo, but it lost money. He then prepared another one, to recover his money, but lost more. With only $1,000 in savings remaining, he accepted a job from a grocery store owner, and within two weeks was made manager. After only six months, however, he left this post to begin his career in automobile sales.

Appleway Chevrolet was located in Dishman in a small two-car showroom at the corner of Appleway (now Sprague Avenue) and Argonne Road. (The name Appleway—given to the continuation of Sprague Avenue east of the city limits—was derived from the numerous orchards that dotted the Spokane Valley. It was changed to Sprague Avenue after several ruinous Depression years forced most valley orchardists out of business.)

After only a year in the business, John Pring and a partner bought out his employer. On May 1, 1929, the dealership was theirs. All appeared well. During a

Substantial remodeling and additions to the Sprague Avenue facility were completed in 1969.

This view of Appleway Chevrolet's current location on Sprague Avenue was taken about 1950.

Jack Pring poses next to the firm's delivery truck in the 1950s.

25-day period in July, Pring himself sold twenty-three cars. But six months' time established Pring and his partner's incompatibility, and Pring bought him out. Now he had to succeed, or face default on borrowed funds from either the former dealer or the ex-partner.

Under Pring's ownership the Appleway Chevrolet dealership increased in value, and Pring kept making payments, despite a number of adversities. The stock market crash of October 31, 1929, cast a shadow over America's financial future, but Spokane's economy was not affected until nearly a year later. In 1930 the bank closures commenced. The first of three that cost Pring money came just fifteen minutes after he made a large deposit. Ultimately he recovered about twenty cents on the dollar.

In 1932 Chevrolet unexpectedly cancelled his franchise. Though the manufacturer wouldn't say why at the time, Pring later found the explanation in the hidden financial misdealings of a former associate. Pring took the news in stride, and for nearly a year sold Dodge and Plymouth cars, plus dozens of Chevrolets from distressed dealers who sold them to Appleway at prices below cost. What could have been a disaster turned out well in the end, with Chevrolet soon asking Pring to resume his dealership.

By 1941 Pring's business had outgrown the original showroom, and he moved to new quarters at the present location at East 8500 Sprague Avenue. The move coincided with Chevrolet's 1942-model announcement day in late September. But within three months the United States was at war, and new-car dealers began a three-year famine as supplies were exhausted. Fortunately, Pring knew horses from his rodeo days, and found the U.S. government a ready buyer of barely broken remounts for European-theater operations.

War-related industries also gave Pring an entry into local real estate development. He built houses for aluminum workers on forty acres at Millwood, and invested the profits in a new Dishman bank that opened in 1943. Other wartime ventures included dealing in farm equipment and even Cessna aircraft, a business at which Pring acknowledges he lost money.

During the postwar period demand for automobiles at first outstripped production capacity, and Appleway Chevrolet's business prospered. By 1955 John Pring's son Jack returned from a stint in the service and assumed managerial duties at Appleway. Later in the decade the family-run businesses, which included at one time as many as three Idaho ranches, were given corporate identities. The principals now include three generations of Pring family members, including Jack's three sons, John, Tim, and Bradley, and Jack's sister, Donna Gillis. The Pring businesses employ nearly 500 persons.

In 1980 the family acquired Playfair racetrack in Spokane. It is managed by Jack and son Bradley, while Tim has become general manager of Appleway Chevrolet. Appleway also became a Toyota dealer in 1982, and acquired Anderson Subaru in 1984. Meanwhile, Jack's elder son John carries on the family tradition by operating a Chevrolet, Datsun, and recreational-vehicle dealership in Lewiston.

R.A. PEARSON COMPANY

R.A. "Lefty" Pearson, founder of R.A. Pearson Company.

R.A. "Lefty" Pearson was employed as packaging superintendent at a Spokane brewery in the early 1950s when he realized that machinery could erect cardboard six-pack carriers more efficiently than manual labor. It was this notion, and a large dose of inventiveness and determination, that brought forth a multimillion-dollar Spokane-based packaging machinery firm with worldwide sales.

The origins of the firm were modest. Starting out in his basement garage, Lefty Pearson designed and built a machine that used vacuum-operated suction cups to set up cardboard six-pack bottle carriers. The device was an instant success, and soon Pearson was filling orders from other northwest brewers and soft-drink bottlers.

The business that Pearson founded in 1955 quickly outgrew his basement garage. Its next location was a small building at South 12 Division Street, followed by a larger facility at East 304 Second Avenue. Since 1977 it has been located in a 70,000-square-foot plant built on a 24-acre West Plains lot near the Spokane International Airport.

Pearson's company was quick to find favor with international customers. While still operating from the basement garage, a German brewer from Munich learned of the machine and contacted Pearson. A sale and a satisfied customer helped to boost additional overseas orders. The company's international market now includes firms in Canada, Europe, Asia, Mexico, South America, and South Africa.

From automated six-pack bottle-carrier erectors, the R.A. Pearson Company expanded into packaging machines designed for food and beverage containers as well as other products. Its machines now form and seal corrugated cardboard cartons and trays, insert box partitions, and pack a variety of products.

The firm employs approximately 100 people in Spokane, including an engineering department dedicated to product improvement and to custom application and design work for customers whose needs are not met by the company's more than twenty-five standard production models of packaging machinery.

The success of the R.A. Pearson Company is a testimony to the strength and vision of its founder, whose efforts on its behalf never flagged, despite a terminal illness diagnosed more than twelve years before his death in 1971. The family-owned business has maintained its position as an industry leader since 1971, through the efforts of able associates and employees.

The home of R.A. Pearson Company at West 8120 Sunset Highway, Spokane.

KERSHAW'S

The main floor of Kershaw's "businessperson's department store."

In 1900, when Fred L. Kershaw began offering office equipment to the Spokane business community, he sold products from a store called Western Typewriter, whose floor space measured a meager six by ten feet. Today the successor company, known as Kershaw's since 1923, styles itself the "businessperson's department store" and boasts more than 72,000 square feet of floor space in downtown and branch locations.

A Massachusetts native, Kershaw arrived in Spokane in 1889 and worked in a bank before opening his first store at West 810 Riverside Avenue. The office products business soon outgrew this location, and by 1908 Kershaw was settled in his third store on this same street. At the end of World War I the business moved to the West 600 block of Sprague Avenue, and by 1925 occupied a new building that housed the concern for more than fifty years. In 1980 Kershaw's moved across the street to its present location in the Seafirst Block at the corner of Sprague and Wall—a move delayed two weeks when Mount St. Helens covered Spokane with inches of machinery-stopping ash. The firm opened a Spokane Valley branch in 1982 and opened another retail store, at North 7307 Division, in 1984. Also that year the firm opened Contact Furnishings and Design at Second and Cowley.

The interior of Kershaw's Empire State Building location on West Riverside Avenue, circa 1925. Pictured are Earl Ashtedt, Gil Swanson, Olaf Gilbertson, and George Swanson.

Kershaw's has a long tradition of developing talent within the organization. Its second president was Charles D. Yenney, husband of Mildred Kershaw, the founder's daughter. Yenney, who was born to a pioneer family—his father arrived in the Walla Walla area by wagon train in 1860—began at the store as a salesman/bookkeeper and assumed its leadership in 1952. The next president of the company was Wesley Melior, who purchased the business in 1962. His retirement in 1973 ended a 43-year-long career at Kershaw's. The present owner of Kershaw's is Rudy Cozzetto, a Spokane native, who began employment with the firm in 1955. He became vice-president in 1966 and president in 1973.

Kershaw's has grown dramatically in recent years in both sales volume and number of employees. With a staff now numbering more than eighty, Kershaw's serves eastern Washington, Idaho, and western Montana. The enterprise prides itself as a one-stop shop for business products, with sales and service of office machines, office furniture, a full range of office, engineering, and art supplies, and office design and printing services. In terms of sales, Kershaw's presently ranks nationally in the top 3 percent of office supply companies. Its size enables it to serve clients in Alaska, Canada, and nationwide whose attempts to find certain products locally have failed.

Much has changed at the venture Fred Kershaw founded at the turn of the century. Where originally deliveries were made on bicycles, a fleet of four trucks now make the rounds. And the ink and ledger accounting systems of the past have succumbed to the computer age. Yet there is still evident at Kershaw's a dedication transmitted to the generation from the founder. The tradition is expressed in Fred Kershaw's motto, recalled by his daughter, Mildred Yenney, "to give the customer the best possible service in the shortest time."

SACRED HEART MEDICAL CENTER

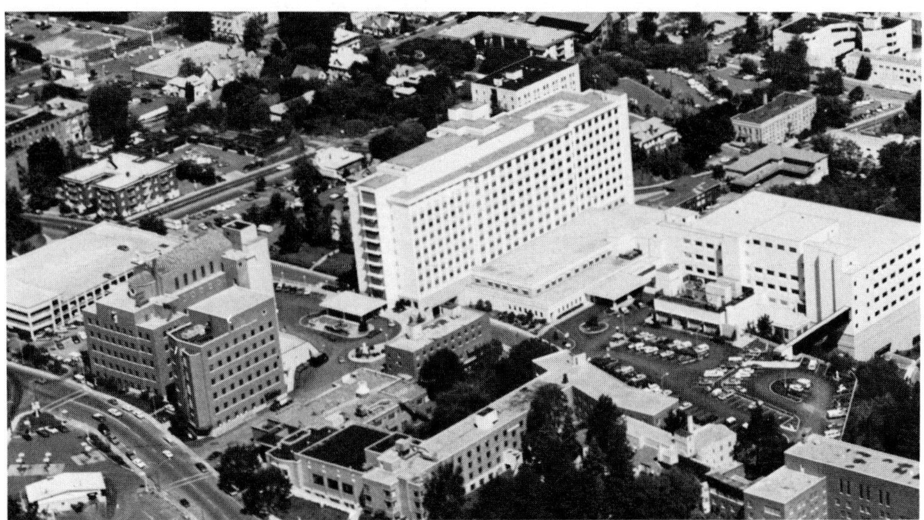

The Sacred Heart Medical Center in 1984, with the new East Addition housing rehabilitation, psychiatric, and outpatient services.

The origins of Spokane's most venerable hospital may be found in the charitable mission of the French-Canadian Sisters of Providence, who first arrived in the Washington Territory in 1856. Answering a call from the Bishop of Nisqually, Mother Joseph and her Sisters of Charity of Providence worked as pioneer care-givers, establishing more than two dozen schools and hospitals throughout the Northwest.

In Spokane, as at her first foundation at Fort Vancouver, Washington, Mother Joseph served as both architect and construction supervisor—and sometimes carpenter, building inspector, and fund raiser. Within a year of her arrival with Sister Joseph Arimathea in 1886, a 31-bed hospital opened at the corner of Trent (now Spokane Falls Boulevard) and Browne on a two-block lot purchased for $2,000. By 1888 the facility had a medical staff of six and had doubled its patient capacity. The Sacred Heart tradition of growing with the community had begun.

National recognition of Mother Joseph's charitable work came in 1980, three-quarters of a century after her death, when she joined Marcus Whitman as Washington's other representative in the National Statuary Hall in Washington, D.C. Her likeness was recreated in bronze by noted sculptor Felix de Weldon. She was the first nun and only the fifth American woman to be so honored.

The flames of Spokane's great fire in 1889 spared the original Sacred Heart Hospital, which continued to serve area residents into the early years of the twentieth century. The march of progress was less yielding, however, as the Sisters of Providence sold the site to Jim Hill, who paid $310,000 to use the land for railway right-of-way. But by the time his Great Northern Railway reached Havermale Island in 1910, a new facility at the Medical Center's present Eighth Avenue and Browne Street location was ready to occupy. This 300-bed hospital was a welcome addition in Spokane, which by 1910 had grown to more than 100,000 residents.

As the city grew during the first decades of the twentieth century, so did its residents' needs for increasingly sophisticated medical care. Sacred Heart Hospital contributed to the training of nurses and medical professionals through its nursing school, internship program, and special technical schools.

As early as 1898 the Sisters of Providence opened a school of nursing at the hospital in order to provide trained personnel for a patient population that had grown too large for the Sisters alone to care for personally. The school prepared nurses for medical service until area hospitals abandoned in-house programs in favor of university-trained nurses in the mid-1970s.

By the late teens hospitals had begun to organize their service

The original Sacred Heart Hospital, built by Mother Joseph at Trent and Browne streets in 1886, is the current site of the Sheraton Hotel.

Sacred Heart Hospital, at Eighth Avenue and Browne Street, in 1915.

functions into departments. The first at Sacred Heart was the radiology department, whose home in 1919 was a single room in a corner of the surgery area. Electronic treatments quickly increased in sophistication, and in 1926 Sacred Heart introduced a high-voltage therapy machine in its X-ray department.

The field of anesthesiology had made significant strides by the 1930s. At Sacred Heart Hospital medical internships were established by 1931 to educate physicians, and in 1937 the School of Anesthesia was founded, joining a School of Medical Technology, which had been established five years earlier.

After World War II Sacred Heart Hospital continued to grow with the community. In 1947 it opened a new nursing school, and in 1950 established physical therapy and emergency service departments. The first open-heart surgery performed in Spokane was done at the facility in 1959, and three years later the hospital became home to the Inland Empire Artificial Kidney Center. Just five years later Sacred Heart pioneered in home dialysis for kidney patients.

Yet despite its prominence in the Spokane medical community, Sacred Heart Hospital and the Sisters of Providence faced a difficult decision in the late 1960s. The hospital's physical plant had become inadequate, and no longer met revised codes for fireproofing nor provided sufficient electrical facilities. The choice was to rebuild or to close.

The decision was not easily reached. The Sisters of Providence recognized that changes in governmental policies increasingly affected the way in which they could provide medical services to the community. And some voices suggested that the Sisters might serve the needy more directly without the administrative responsibilities of a major medical institution.

The Sisters assessed Spokane's needs and the ability of others to satisfy them without Sacred Heart. After much deliberation, the Sisters concluded that the hospital was essential. The decision to borrow money for the rebuilding took the Sisters of Providence, in the words of the present administrator, Sister Peter Claver, "back to our historic commitment" to fill unmet needs, and to refuse no one, regardless of ability to pay.

Since the dedication in 1971 of the $35-million Sacred Heart Medical Center, few have doubted that the Sisters of Providence made a wise decision. In the past decade the institution has continued to provide leadership in the Spokane medical community, most recently with the opening of a new psychiatric unit with a portion of its facilities dedicated to child and adolescent mental health care. Sacred Heart's impact in Spokane is far greater than that which can be measured in numbers of dollars, beds, and staff, but it is Spokane's second-largest private employer.

Sacred Heart Medical Center reflects in its policies and priorities the original commitment of the Sisters of Providence. There are fifteen Sister members now, dwarfed in number by the professional and support staff of Sacred Heart, but the Christian mission of caring for those in need is reflected daily both in the Sisters' own ministry and in the medical attention given by the entire Sacred Heart community.

PRODUCE SUPPLY COMPANY

Harry R. Cooper, now retired, in 1969.

Spokane's leading institutional produce distributor, Produce Supply Company, can trace its founding to a classified advertisement placed in a Spokane newspaper shortly after World War II. At that time Clark McKee sought a partner to help him operate a retail fruit stand. He chose Harry Cooper from among thirty-two respondents, and the pair set up shop on Sprague Avenue. The first month they split a twenty-five dollar profit three ways: one share each for the partners and the third to their landlord for rent.

Harry R. Cooper was no stranger to the food industry. As a teenager he had helped his father, a logging-camp cook, during summers, and later put in a four-month stint as a railroad crew cook. Though the Depression put many people out of work, he decided to visit Armour Meat's big Spokane packing plant. In the personnel office dozens of men were milling around. As he approached the counter, a voice inquired if he wanted to start working. After a month on the job, Harry asked why he had been so fortunate. "Because you looked like you wanted to work" was the unambiguous reply!

After a year together, Harry Cooper persuaded his partner to begin a wholesale operation. He was convinced that the business would succeed, because restaurant owners then were poorly served by produce vendors. Retailers typically sold their best produce to retail customers, Harry recalls, "and sold second-grade produce out the back door to restaurants." Harry Cooper saw an opportunity, and Produce Supply Company was established at West 1116 Ide Street. The operation was an immediate success.

After Clark McKee retired in 1949, the business continued to grow, so Harry brought in Harry L. Meyers in 1952 as a one-quarter-interest partner, and arranged to have Eddie and Seiko Edamatsu produce and sell their prepared salad mix (Eddie's Salad Mix) at Produce Supply. But Harry Cooper's biggest innovation was with potatoes. He saw food wasted by abrasive peelers, and remembered how his father had taught him to take razor-thin shavings from spuds in the logging camp. Using production-line techniques learned at Armour, Produce Supply Company soon was selling ready-to-cook hash browns and fries. Such innovation in the early 1950s made Harry Cooper a true pioneer in the food-service industry. Recognition of his leadership came in 1962, when the Spokane County Hotel and Restaurant Council honored him with its first-ever Supplier of the Year award.

By 1963 Produce Supply Company had outgrown its West Ide Street quarters. Land was acquired and the firm moved to its present location at East 919 Trent. Eight additions later, the concern now occupies 50,000 square feet, and leases another 25,000 to a cash-and-carry outlet. Produce Supply Company's sixty employees distribute fresh, canned, and frozen fruits and vegetables to institutional clients in the greater Spokane area. This includes ninety tons of potatoes per week, of which four tons a day are processed at the company plant.

Harry Cooper retired from Produce Supply Company in 1981. The firm is now owned and operated by his three sons, John, Pat, and Jim Cooper.

Partners Harry Cooper (third from left) and Harry Meyers (right) join employees at the potato peeling assembly line in this 1953 photo.

VERN W. JOHNSON & SONS, INC.

Vern W. Johnson was just five years old when he started acquiring first-hand knowledge of the construction business. His father was a carpenter in Salina, Kansas, who often acted as his own general contractor. Customers would point to a house and say, "I want one like that." A trip to the lumberyard got construction under way, with young Vern applying lath while his three older brothers helped their father with heavier work.

Vern Johnson's skill with his hands was complemented by a keen mind (he advanced to state-level math contests as a high school student), so his family staked him to a college education. By 1932 he had graduated from what is now Kansas State University with a degree in architectural engineering and, despite the Depression, landed a job in the construction industry. It only paid forty cents an hour, but it was work!

Through the 1930s Johnson worked at times with the Army Corps of Engineers and then Kansas construction firms, whose fortunes improved through a double dose of pump priming from President Roosevelt's Public Works Administration and Presidential aspirant (and Kansas governor) Alf Landon's state work projects. His work for the Busboom and Rauh Company provided him a tour of nine midwestern and western states, bringing him as close to Spokane as Grangeville, Idaho, in 1941. By the end of the war Johnson had decided to make the Inland Empire his home.

Working initially from the basement of his house in Spokane, Vern Johnson soon established himself in the local contracting community. One of his first projects was the W.P. Fuller Company building on East Boone—a job he almost lost when that company's Art Chase told Johnson that he had dealt with another contractor for the past twenty-five years. Johnson's quick reply, "Mr. Chase, I'm going to be here for the next twenty-five years," so impressed his client that he got the job.

Vern Johnson's business grew steadily from that time on. In 1947 the organization constructed its present headquarters at North 601 Cedar and subsequently became a leading Spokane general contractor for commercial, industrial, and institutional building. In 1958 the firm added the words "& Sons" to its name when the first of two sons to join the business came aboard.

Vern W. Johnson, founder of the general contracting business that bears his name.

During nearly four decades in Spokane, Vern Johnson has contributed both to his industry and to civic causes. In the early 1950s he served as president of the Construction Council, and once helped settle an important carpenters' strike by agreeing to a five-cent addition to hourly rates of pay. An active business leader in Spokane, Johnson led the YMCA relocation effort and worked hard to make Expo '74 a community success as chairman of site development.

SPOKANE STEEL FOUNDRY AND SPOKANE METAL PRODUCTS
Division of Spokane Industries, Inc.

Spokane Steel's foundry, circa 1960.

In 1965 Spokane Steel Foundry moved to the Spokane Industrial Park, where it occupies over 240,000 square feet of space in three buildings.

Spokane's close proximity to the Coeur d'Alene mining district played a key role in the early years of Spokane Steel Foundry, the company John C. Tenold began with three partners in 1952. The nearby silver mines provided a ready market for cast-steel mill balls, and John Tenold's education as a metallurgical engineer and brief experience as a hard-rock miner in California gave him the knowledge to meet the need. Soon the firm was casting steel parts in a 4,000-square-foot building on Mission Street near Fancher Road.

Spokane Steel Foundry's business increased significantly in 1956, when it became a sole-source supplier of replacement track roller guards for the Caterpillar Tractor Company. The cast part was an improvement over fabricated steel, and Spokane Steel Foundry's agreement to sell it only through Caterpillar channels made that company's dealers happy. With things going so well, John Tenold was just a little apprehensive when Caterpillar executives called him in for an unscheduled meeting. He soon learned that Caterpillar's only concern was that his prices were too low—they wanted him to remain profitable and in business for a long time. They needn't have worried, as Spokane Steel Foundry added additional clients whose orders for truck castings, winch parts, specialty railroad items, marine parts, and crusher wear parts helped the firm prosper.

This steady growth caused Spokane Steel Foundry to outgrow its original plant. In 1965 it moved to the Spokane Industrial Park, where it now occupies over 240,000 square feet of space in three buildings, employs over 200 people, and sports automated control systems and modern pollution-control equipment.

In 1970 Spokane Steel Foundry acquired a local manufacturer of rock-crushing equipment. This high-production, vertical-shaft impact crusher quickly became popular, and soon gained the number-one market position for this type of machine. Though this division was sold in 1983, a Minnesota manufacturer continues to market the product, throughout the world, as the "Spokane Crusher."

In 1978 the corporation added another division, Spokane Metal Products. This venture, which makes wine and fertilizer tanks and other products from rolls of stainless steel, has earned a reputation for its quality throughout the western United States.

In 1981 the firm coined a new corporate name, Spokane Industries, to emphasize the multidivisional nature of its business. The company continues to market its products under the names of its operating divisions, Spokane Steel Foundry and Spokane Metal Products.

The civic spirit of Spokane Industries' executives is indicated through John C. Tenold's tenure as past president of the Spokane Symphony Society and the United Way, and in the firm's 1973 role in casting a sculpture to honor Vietnam POWs and MIAs.

The last of John C. Tenold's original five partners was bought out in 1973, and Tenold ran the enterprise with his four sons—Bob, Jack, Greg, and Tyrus—until his retirement in 1984. The operations of the company are now managed by Bob and Greg Tenold.

KEY TRONIC CORPORATION

When Key Tronic Corporation founder Lewis G. Zirkle resigned his position with a north Idaho microswitch maker in the late 1960s, he thought he saw but two choices: look for another job back east or go fishing. Naturally, he went fishing. His catch included the seminal ideas for a business now recognized as the leading manufacturer of computer keyboards and other data entry devices.

Zirkle was well prepared to seize the opportunity that the burgeoning market in small computers presented. He describes his twenty-four years with General Electric as a continual enhancement of his education, and credits his nine years of managing small businesses for imparting additional operating know-how.

The firm began with Lewis Zirkle and just four others in the fall of 1969. In November the company designed its first keyboard; in January 1970 the product passed its first tests and was shipped by April. That first year the fledgling enterprise produced 5,000 keyboards and grossed $.5 million. The pace hasn't slowed since.

At first Key Tronic sold keyboards exclusively to computer makers. There were many companies just starting up in the early 1970s, all thirsty for keyboards. A significant break for Key Tronic came in 1981, when it developed a low-profile keyboard. This design was dictated by West German labor standards that stipulated a 25-percent wage premium beginning in 1985 for employees not provided with ergonomic equipment. Ergo, Europe began demanding qualified keyboards, and Key Tronic had a head start providing them. The low-profile design has since become an industry standard.

Lewis G. Zirkle, founder of Key Tronic Corporation.

When the company decided that it would manufacture other data input devices, new markets opened. Now Key Tronic supplies some products directly to end-users. The increasing development of "intelligent keyboards" led to the introduction in 1984 of additional data entry devices. Such products as optical character devices, hand-held "mice," and voice entry systems have maintained Key Tronic's technological leadership.

Key Tronic Corporation employs more than 2,500 persons at five locations: Spokane, Newport, and Cheney, Washington, and overseas in Litlebergen, Norway, and in Taiwan. The corporate headquarters in Spokane was relocated in June 1984 to a new building near the original plant site at the Spokane Industrial Park. The company is studying expansion of manufacturing facilities to Ireland to help serve the European market and to meet an expected 30-percent annual growth rate.

The first fifteen years of Key Tronic's existence have seen tremendous growth, which the firm attributes to the quality of its people. Key Tronic management was an early advocate of "quality circle" teamwork, and the company fosters employee development through continuing education and promotion from within. The results are impressive: a Spokane-based corporation with annual sales exceeding $100 million and a leading position in a constantly expanding high-technology industry.

EZ LOADER BOAT TRAILERS

The current board of directors of the firm is composed of (top row, left to right) David Thielman, vice-president; Marc Johnson, vice-president; Randy Johnson, vice-president; and Craig Thielman, vice-president. Seated are Lawrence N. Johnson, president; and William A. Thielman, secretary.

Though Lawrence N. Johnson professes Spokane to be "the worst place in the world to build boat trailers"—due to its remoteness from larger markets—the business that he began here in the early 1950s has overcome that disadvantage and now leads the industry in gross sales, with an annual production approaching 50,000 units.

But first, Larry Johnson and his partners, Bill Thielman and Wendel Holton, had to decide what business they were really in.

The three men had each contributed $500 to establish a body shop in Hillyard in 1946. It must have been the quality of their body and fender work that attracted customers, because neither their quarters (a converted dairy building) nor their location (on Wabash east of Market) were considered advantageous.

It was the search for a better location that prompted the partners' acquisition in 1951 of a welding business at North 637 Hamilton. The deal was contingent upon the previous owners agreeing to teach Larry Johnson their trade. They did, and for the next seven years Johnson expanded the business of Modern Welding and Machine Works and Holton and Thielman carried on at the body shop, which remained in Hillyard.

Not long afterward Johnson used his design skills to construct trailers, first to transport Holton's fishing boat, then to haul building materials to a lakeside cabin site. Others became interested, and soon Johnson was building a few custom boat trailers and repairing some shipped from Connecticut for sale at a local marina. Soon the marina asked Johnson to make them here, and ultimately purchased some 250 of this model.

Johnson's early experiences whetted his appetite for the trailer business—still very much a sideline—and stimulated his creativity. By 1953 he had introduced enough improvements to give his boat trailer a name. Because of a tilt-tongue that facilitated launching and loading, it became his first trailer to bear a name: EZ Loader.

It took five years for Johnson to produce 1,000 trailers. By this time his partners had installed the body shop in a new addition to the Hamilton Street structure. The facility strained to house both operations but the market for boat trailers continued to improve. A new body shop built next door in 1963 finally liberated the original welding shop for manufacturing only. EZ Loader became a substantial supplier to Northwest dealers.

The major turning point came in 1961, when Johnson patented his innovative self-adjusting all-roller trailer. Chicago trade show appearances in 1970 and 1971 gave EZ Loader a national market. Its success led to the sale of the body shop operations, and Johnson and Thielman and their sons (Holton sold his interest following a heart attack in 1968) now dedicate their time exclusively to boat trailers.

With growth came expansion into two facilities vacated in 1968 and 1970 by a truck line and American Oil. These buildings across Hamilton Street became the EZ Loader assembly line where 200 employees form, paint, and package trailer parts for assembly at points of sale throughout North America and around the world.

THE CRESCENT

The Crescent constructed its own building at Riverside and Wall in 1898 (left) and still occupies the same location today (above).

August 5, 1889, was an unusual opening business day for Spokane Falls' new dry goods store. In the preceding twenty-four hours most of the town's business district had burned to the ground. Five days after the fire a news article in the *Spokane Falls Review* noted that the proprietors of the store were receiving goods daily "and are selling at regular prices." The owners, it stated, "should be encouraged, as they have come here to stay and will build up a fine class of trade."

The newcomer to Spokane's business community was Robert B. Paterson, a partner in the mercantile trade with Captain J.M. Comstock in Charles City, Iowa. Sent by Comstock to Spokane, Paterson arranged for sixteen- by ninety-foot quarters in the newly constructed Crescent Block—which the great fire's flames spared. From the outset the business took its name from the shape of the building's facade.

Within two years Captain Comstock and two valued employees from Iowa, James L. Paine and Eugene A. Shadle, had joined Paterson in Spokane. In 1893 The Crescent was strong enough to weather the economic panic that swept the land. According to Captain Comstock's daughter, "The Crescent survived because the people of Spokane Falls had come to know that my father was always fair, that he loved everyone, and treated all alike."

An occupant of several leased premises during its first decade, The Crescent purchased sixty-eight feet of frontage at Riverside and Wall in 1898 and commenced construction of its own building. In 1903 it acquired facilities on Main Street for a wholesale arm, the Spokane Dry Goods Co., established in 1895.

By 1909 The Crescent employed 300 persons. Further expansion was necessary, first to the wholesale quarters facing on Main Street, then to an adjacent plot of land at the corner of Main and Wall. By 1919 the first portion of The Crescent's present building had reached its current seven-story height.

The Crescent survived the lean years of the Great Depression as a family-owned business. Directed first by Comstock and Paterson, then by Paine and Shadle, the firm drew upon the talents of Mrs. E.A. Shadle—Captain Comstock's daughter—and Robert A. Paterson—son of Robert B. Paterson—who led the company from 1939 until 1966. Robert L. Paterson was named president in 1966 following his father's retirement.

In 1969 The Crescent became a subsidiary of the Marshall Field Company of Chicago. This group was purchased in 1982 by British American Tobacco-U.S.—an international firm that provides administrative, marketing, and purchasing resources to its stores while leaving them a large measure of local operating independence.

Today The Crescent is the employer of more than 800 residents of Spokane, and the full-line department store of preference for many Spokanites and out-of-town customers.

THE HASKINS COMPANY

Company founder Roy Haskins (right) with son Sterling (center) and grandson Scott.

When Roy Haskins arrived in Spokane from Oklahoma in 1948 with his wife, Connie, he had "a welding machine, a car, two small children, and lots of ambition." No doubt his welding skill and ambition, combined with a personality and character that inspired confidence, accounted for much of his early success. Hard work, inventiveness, and a helpful family also contributed to the transformation of the small welding shop into a multi-million-dollar general contracting firm and steel products company.

Roy Haskins learned welding at an early age in Cushing, Oklahoma, where his father plied the trade in local oil fields. He studied technical-vocational subjects for two years at Oklahoma A&M, and used his talents to aid the war effort during the early 1940s.

Transplanted to Spokane, Roy set up shop in rented space at East 34 Trent Avenue. Though Connie had not intended to work, the business became a family operation early on. Roy said he needed help "at the beginning," recalls Connie—who has remained active in the firm ever since. Other family members who migrated to Spokane after the war also pitched in.

Every job was important, especially at the outset. During the cold winter of 1949 Roy and a recently arrived cousin put their torches to work to thaw frozen pipes. On one such mission the temperature dipped so low that even gasoline wouldn't ignite. And to top it off, when the work was done the motel owner north of Spokane wouldn't pay his bill.

The present location of The Haskins Company in 1952, before additions and remodeling.

As a general contractor, The Haskins Company got its start in 1949 with the construction of a storage tank for a grain cooperative at Hanson Station, west of Wilbur, Washington. In these early years Roy designed his products at night and sold them during the day to farmers who appreciated the time he took with them as well as his quiet manner. During this period Roy patented a jacking system for erecting storage tanks that resulted in more efficient construction. He also received a patent for a portable tilt-bin used for fertilizer storage.

With the help of grain growers who could be counted on to pay their bills, the company grew steadily during the early 1950s. The year 1954 was particularly good for business, and the following year The Haskins Steel Company was established as a separate corporate entity, providing sales of steel products and steel fabrication service to welding shops or large industrial shops. The Haskins Company retained its general contracting business, specializing in grain storage, feed mills, seed plants, and commercial and office buildings.

The two firms now employ approximately twelve persons in management, sales, and clerical roles, with about 100 nonunion hourly workers—though as many as 150 or 200 more are needed for construction work.

The Haskins Company has grown to its present size without

The present Haskins Steel Company plant on East Main Avenue.

incurring debt. More than once its practice of saving during good years to prepare for leaner ones has given it an edge over competitors. Roy and Connie Haskins also credit the application of Christian principles to company operations with helping them in business.

Once, Connie relates, the firm sorely needed work and was competing for a contract near the Washington-Oregon border. But the family's prayers and those of fellow Baptists at their church seemed unanswered. Later they learned that the successful bidder had lost money on the job, and in the meantime they had landed a profitable one on the other side of the Columbia River.

As Haskins grew it began to serve customers farther afield. One way to continue to provide personal service was to use a company plane that could land even at small airfields. In 1955 Roy became a pilot and the firm began to cover its Washington, Oregon, Idaho, and Montana territory by aircraft. And Roy has been joined at the controls since 1965 by his son, Sterling.

Sterling Haskins got an early initiation into the business. At age twelve, with permission from Labor and Industries, he was allowed in the shop and did such chores as sweeping, cleaning iron, and then welding. He was only fourteen when he worked on his first job, and by age eighteen was employed on a crew erecting tanks. After two years at Washington State University, Sterling started working at bookkeeping, but soon found that his calling was sales. Within a few years he had contributed to the company's first gross of $1.5 million annual sales. His mother remembers that he fairly burst with pride—only to be brought down to earth when Haskins' profit that year amounted to a modest $1,500.

Since then the firm has posted better results, and counts among its projects some major Northwest grain facilities. Haskins constructed both a 1.6-million-bushel flathouse in Kennewick in 1975, and the largest corn-storage facility in the Northwest, a 4.5-million-bushel structure near Umatilla, in 1980.

The Haskins Company built the largest corn-storage facility in the Pacific Northwest near Umatilla for U&I Inc. in 1980.

Over the years the Haskinses have employed four generations of family members. In the early days both Roy's and Connie's fathers helped out. Later contributions came from one daughter, and recently Sterling's son, Scott, has assumed a management role after completing studies in accounting at Seattle Pacific University.

McVAY BROTHERS

McVay Brothers' office and warehouse at North 3106 Argonne Road, Spokane, in 1959.

It has been nearly fifty years since a McVay brother agreed to accept a sheep or cow as payment for roofing and siding work, though the Spokane company that bears the family name has helped prolong the life of many an Inland Empire residence, both on farms and in cities and towns from the Rockies to the Cascades. Founded during the Depression when cash was scarce, the firm has always adapted itself to changing economic times. At one time providing a livelihood for as many as six McVay brothers and dozens of administrative and hourly employees, it now serves a less far-flung clientele under second-generation McVay management.

The brothers who built the reputation of the enterprise were sons of a Spokane-area postman brought here at the age of four in 1883. The second eldest son, J.D. McVay, began doing business from an office in the Hutton Building in 1935, but soon moved to locations on East Sprague and East Trent as his younger brothers joined the firm: Harry in the late 1930s, and Warren and Add in the early 1940s. In 1955 the company became a partnership of Harry and Warren McVay, and in January 1958 it moved to its present quarters at North 3106 Argonne.

Success did not come without a lot of long hours and hard work. During the 1950s and 1960s Harry and Warren McVay spent most Mondays through Thursdays canvassing out-of-town customers. The days often began with an 8 a.m. farm stop and usually didn't finish until 10 p.m. or later. Fridays in Spokane were hectic times when order processing and crew scheduling took priority.

McVay Brothers' flair for advertising is exhibited on this Spokane city bus of the early 1950s.

But the fast pace had its human side, too. Neither partner will forget the numerous friends they made throughout the Inland Empire. Nor will communities like Rockford soon forget such McVay deeds as the roof repair done for a widow victimized by a fly-by-night operator. And more than one Republic citizen may recall the harrowing spectacle of McVay's application of siding to the Republic Hotel from the top of sixty-foot ladders. (The company now uses more secure means for reaching heights!)

Still, Harry McVay found time to serve as a trustee of Whitworth College, as president of the Union Gospel Mission, and as a leading member of other community organizations.

While the mainstay of the McVay Brothers' business was always residential siding and roofing, the firm has also sold roofing, siding, windows, and awnings supplies, sometimes to customers as far away as Canada and Alaska.

Around 1970 McVay Brothers became the first Spokane area roofing and siding company to advertise on television. The commercials worked so well that the firm strained to fill customer demand. Now, since the retirement of Harry and Warren McVay in the early 1980s, the business has scaled back roofing and siding operations to a smaller radius from Spokane while promoting do-it-yourself sales and a line of retail paints at its Millwood location. Family ownership of McVay Brothers continues today under the capable leadership of Harry McVay's son, Harrison E. McVay, Jr.

KAISER ALUMINUM & CHEMICAL CORPORATION

Henry J. Kaiser often traveled without elegance but seldom without style. The year was 1946 at the Trentwood rolling mill. That's Henry J. tipping his hat to the photographer.

The road that Kaiser Aluminum's founder, Henry J. Kaiser, followed to success as an industrialist features Spokane on more than one of its milestones. It was to Spokane that the young New York native came, full of ambition, in 1906. It was here that Kaiser's son, Edgar, was born. It was in the Spokane Valley and neighboring community of Mead that Kaiser acquired the company's first aluminum reduction and rolling mills shortly after the end of World War II.

From the moment Henry Kaiser arrived in 1906, he demonstrated an unusual character and entrepreneurial spirit. After hearing for two weeks that James C. McGowan had no job openings in his hardware store, Kaiser finally persuaded the local merchant to let him polish and sell a tarnished pile of silverware. Kaiser didn't mention that his plan included commissioning thirty young women to apply the elbow grease, but the results were what really mattered. He sold the merchandise, delivered a profit, and earned a place on McGowan's payroll.

Before leaving Spokane, Kaiser picked up some experience in the sand and gravel business. He then departed for British Columbia, where his Vancouver-based roadway paving company underbid competitors up and down the West Coast. Once he had a contract, Kaiser put his mind to work figuring out how to make it profitable. Generally, he succeeded.

Kaiser's ability to organize people to get jobs done efficiently enabled him in the late 1920s and 1930s to tackle some of the biggest construction challenges of the century. After a dam-building apprenticeship in the Sierra Nevada, Kaiser turned to less well-charted territory: a piece of a 200-mile-long road the length of Cuba, and then participation in the construction of the mighty Hoover, Bonneville, and Grand Coulee dams.

During the hectic early 1940s Kaiser helped maximize wartime industrial output. After the war Kaiser saw a future for aluminum where critics saw only oversupply of metal and facilities. Against the advice of experts, Kaiser acquired surplus plants at Mead and Trentwood, and launched his organization into the aluminum business in 1946. Within a year these facilities had produced 60,000 tons of aluminum and a $5.3-million profit.

Today Kaiser Aluminum is Spokane's largest private-industry employer, providing jobs for about 2,500 people. The company's impact on the local economy is over $320 million annually.

Kaiser's Mead reduction facility is the second largest of the company's four domestic reduction plants. The plant has eight potlines, and its annual rated primary aluminum capacity is 220,000 tons.

At Kaiser's Trentwood mill in the Spokane Valley, a $230-million modernization project has made it the most modern rolling mill in the world. Trentwood is a sheet and plate plant and produces a wide range of semifabricated products.

Kaiser Aluminum & Chemical Corporation is a diversified company with worldwide operations. Yet its primary activity is still aluminum—a focus that Henry J. Kaiser provided when he brought his firm to Spokane and the Northwest in 1946.

R.A. HANSON COMPANY, INC.

Raymond A. Hanson, president.

The corporate headquarters and plant of the R.A. Hanson Company, Inc., are located in this 200,000-square-foot manufacturing facility in Mead.

The R.A. Hanson Company, Inc., is best known as a manufacturer of construction equipment that moves earth and applies concrete, but this description does not do justice to the inventive genius of its president and understates the uniqueness of the firm. This group specializes in accomplishing one-of-a-kind engineering feats. The company works by the motto, "If someone else can do it, let 'em!"

The R.A. Hanson Company got its founding impetus when Raymond Hanson, then enrolled at the University of Idaho in mechanical engineering, dropped out of school. School took up too much of his time, and he had to "go out and do my own thing."

It was natural that this Palouse farm boy would apply his talent first to agriculture. During summers he had worked with combines to bring in the harvest, and knew how inefficient they could be on the steep hillsides of the Palouse countryside. Tilting combines wasted grain and cost farmers money, so a leveling device, operated manually, had been installed at the outboard end of harvesters. The trouble was that it was nearly impossible for an operator to maintain true level.

One of the firm's endeavors was the deep underground basing system jacking station and rotary excavator for the MX missile project for the Department of Defense.

So in 1944 Hanson invented an automatic leveler for combines that had as its heart a mercury switch. He sold 3,000 of the devices direct to farmers, and then began to market his invention to equipment manufacturers. Though his patent expired nearly twenty years ago, Hanson still builds levelers for International Harvester and supplies the control mechanism for the leveler on Allis-Chalmers combines.

The leveling principle later contributed to his success on a Columbia River water-reclamation project in the mid-1950s. A friend who was working on the project asked him to apply his expertise to improving the performance of canal-building machinery. He did, and soon became a manufacturer of advanced-design heavy construction equipment. One system that he developed in the early 1960s allows for in-place casting of large concrete pipes.

A major turning point for Hanson's firm came in 1965, when

he became the major source for large construction machines used to build the 400-mile-long California aqueduct. His excavators trimmed canal slopes to the unparalleled tolerance of one-eighth of an inch, and his concrete-laying equipment provided similar accuracy. Using his machines for all but the first fifteen miles of the project, the prime contractors were able to lay a record 3,000 cubic yards of concrete per day.

The California aqueduct put the R.A. Hanson Company into the big time among heavy-equipment manufacturers and opened up worldwide markets for its canal-building equipment.

Soon after the completion of the California aqueduct project the company moved from Palouse to Spokane. A former Kaiser Aluminum plant in Mead provided a nearly 200,000-square-foot manufacturing facility. The Mead site is now corporate headquarters for the firm, as well as four other corporate entities that specialize in research and development, manufacturing, export sales, mining, and real estate.

This complex of companies grew to maturity during the past two decades as one successful project led to another. In 1971 Hanson developed a self-propelled and automatically controlled machine to clean gravel from canal bottoms for the U.S. Bureau of Reclamation.

The following year brought a singular challenge: to design a 1,900-ton gantry crane to install the Grand Coulee Dam's third power generator. The crane had to be capable of lowering the sixty-foot-wide rotor into its housing within an accuracy tolerance of only one thirty-second of an inch.

This potash-harvesting machine, operating near the Dead Sea, was designed by the R.A. Hanson Company for the Arab Potash Company of Jordan.

The Alaska pipeline provided additional opportunities for innovation, as the R.A. Hanson Company designed and manufactured twelve pipeline back-filling machines for use during construction. It also developed techniques for mixing concrete without the use of rotary drums, a process used for lining deep mine shafts, and a radar-controlled coal auger for thin-seam mining.

The firm's work for the U.S. Bureau of Mines in the 1970s led to Department of Defense contract work on siting alternatives for the MX missile. From the "buried trench" to "multiple-protective shelters" to the "deep underground" proposals, Hanson has worked to develop techniques and machinery to implement America's nuclear defense strategy.

The R.A. Hanson Company made news in 1980 during the hostage crisis with Iran by refusing to honor an urgent plea from that country to supply it with operating and instruction manuals for canal-building equipment purchased by the Shah. The firm told the Iranians that it would consider the request only when the American hostages were released.

Hanson's equipment has been particularly useful in the Middle East. The company has not only sold canal-digging machinery, but has recently developed a potash harvester—a variety of dredge—for Jordan, which by 1984 had three in operation on a total order of seven.

Closer to home Raymond Hanson recently chaired the Washington State University stadium building committee, and also contributed technical expertise and company staff time. The problem, how to enlarge an existing stadium, was solved by lowering the field thirteen feet and adding seats downward. In the bargain, enough soil was moved to make a new baseball field.

The WSU stadium work illustrates the kind of response that customers have come to expect from the R.A. Hanson Company, Inc. Their difficult and unusual problems create Hanson's opportunities.

INLAND POWER & LIGHT COMPANY

The three co-founders of Inland Power & Light Company (left to right), Dan Hopkins, Leo Thams, and Arnold Burgess, are shown in a photo from the early 1950s.

As few as fifty years ago, rural electrification was still a distant dream for most farming families across the United States. It has become a reality since then for nearly all, due in large measure to the New Deal legislation of President Franklin D. Roosevelt and the work of individuals like those who founded Inland Empire Rural Electrification, Inc.—now Inland Power & Light Company—during the dark days of the Depression.

The keys to Inland's contribution to improving the living and working environment of northeastern Washington were vision, hard work, and cooperative effort. These first came together in the persons of Dan Hopkins, Leo Thams, and Arnold Burgess, who refused to accept the oft-stated claim that rural electrification was economically "impossible," and personally convinced many fellow farmers of electricity's benefits.

The cooperative utility they formed was not the first in eastern Washington, but it grew to be the largest. With about 18,000 member families and enough miles of lines to extend from here to Paris, France, it is bigger than any other co-op west of the Mississippi River. The utility began with a promise: five dollars now and electricity within a year. With neighbors often working together to put up lines, the fledgling co-op kept its word and brought the electricity that would soon help to power tools and appliances and light farm homes.

Inland's first electricity was purchased from the Washington Water Power Company, and in 1942 the Bonneville Power Administration started to provide Inland's requirements. Since then Inland has remained an exclusive customer of Bonneville Power Administration electricity.

The growth of Inland's service area slowed during World War II due to materials shortages, but then resumed in the late 1940s and 1950s. The utility now serves customers in portions of eleven Washington and three Idaho counties, including many areas that are now suburban rather than rural in nature.

One of the most challenging tasks the utility has faced was extending service over the summit of Mt. Spokane. This job was completed in 1954, but high winds and heavy winter icing combined to bring the wires down. Even reinforced cross-arms snapped. Finally, Inland decided to lay underground cable—a solution that ended the problems at Mt. Spokane.

The utility attempted at an early date to acquire power generation facilities. By the early 1950s it had foreseen future power needs and advocated joint construction of the Little Goose Dam on the Snake River. But it failed to persuade its partners of the need and couldn't afford it alone. In 1982 Inland signed a twenty-year, full-requirements contract with the Bonneville Power Administration in order to meet its future electrical needs.

Since the 1970s the company has promoted conservation of electricity through home weatherization, and its program has been cited as an example for other utilities by the BPA. Other services to members include a credit union founded in 1961. Organized nearly fifty years ago by and for its members, Inland Power & Light faces the future as it faced the past—cooperatively.

More than 5,300 miles of Inland power lines crisscross rural eastern Washington to bring electricity to remotely located homes.

WASHINGTON TRUST BANK

Washington Trust Bank, founded in 1902, is located in Spokane's financial district in the Washington Trust Financial Center.

The Washington Trust Company was founded in Spokane in 1902. Organized by J. Grier Long, Romie L. Webster, and Martin B. Connelly, the enterprise opened its offices at 115 Mill Street—which was soon renamed Wall Street at Long's suggestion. He thought it only fitting that Spokane's financial thoroughfare should bear the same name as its New York counterpart!

It was a time when eastern financiers, railroad builders, and industrialists were establishing America's giant corporations and amassing huge private fortunes. Locally, railroads and mining projects helped to centralize much Inland Empire wealth in Spokane.

In this period of rapid growth for Spokane the Washington Trust Company prospered. Originally capitalized at $50,000, by 1912 the bank had accumulated assets of one million dollars and moved to a new location at the corner of Post and Riverside.

E.H. Stanton, a successful meat-packing plant operator, sold his business for one million dollars and bought the controlling interest in the bank.

Stanton was a Montanan who had settled in Sprague, thirty-five miles southwest of Spokane, around the turn of the century. There he developed a successful meat-packing business—selling much of his product to railroad and lumber camps. In frontier fashion he dared to take chances, losing on some and gaining on others. It was a character trait that instilled a sense of conservatism in his son, Frederick L. Stanton.

With E.H. Stanton on the board of directors, management of the bank was placed in the hands of Martin Connelly and Frederick Stanton.

The bank thrived under their leadership, and earned an enviable reputation during the Depression when it met every request for withdrawal of funds.

The success of Washington Trust in maintaining the public's faith following the stock market crash of 1929 spurred its growth and led to the purchase of larger quarters at West 715 Sprague Avenue in 1932. By 1941 the bank's assets exceeded ten million dollars.

In 1941 Eugene Enloe, who had replaced Martin Connelly as president after the latter's death in 1932, retired from active management of the bank. The directors then elected Frederick Stanton, who at age fifty-four became the youngest bank president ever in Spokane.

The postwar period provided another period of sustained growth. In 1950 Washington Trust became the first bank in Spokane and the Inland Empire to open a drive-in branch. A year later the firm was officially renamed Washington Trust Bank.

By the early 1960s Washington Trust had expanded its branch-bank system in Spokane to four facilities. Philip H. Stanton succeeded his father as bank president in 1962, and at age thirty-one set a new record for youth in this position.

In the years since 1962 Washington Trust has expanded to a sixteen-branch bank with offices in Spokane and Deer Park, and total assets of approximately $440 million. In 1974 it opened new headquarters, the Washington Trust Financial Center, on the block from Sprague to First and from Post to Wall. In 1979 Philip Stanton became chairman of the board and Thomas L. Perko, president.

GOODALE AND BARBIERI

Louis L. Barbieri (left) and son Donald K., partners in the property-management firm of Goodale and Barbieri.

The property-management firm of Goodale and Barbieri is in some ways a descendant of the pioneer firms of Arthur D. Jones and Martin B. Connelly. Jones' real estate development concern was the training ground for Connelly, who in 1902 became a co-founder of the Washington Trust Company. This venture (now Washington Trust Bank) established a trust department for property management that included clients formerly handled by Connelly and Jones.

After World War I Washington Trust Company employed Frank M. Goodale in the trust department. When the firm decided to shed its property-management section in 1944, Goodale bought it out and called his new enterprise the F.M. Goodale Company. One employee who came with him from Washington Trust was Louis L. Barbieri.

Lou Barbieri was raised in Desmet and Wallace, Idaho. His education included business and law at Gonzaga University—studies he paid for by working at Washington Trust, first as a messenger and then under Goodale in the trust department.

In 1956 Barbieri became Goodale's partner, and the concern assumed its present name of Goodale and Barbieri. Although Goodale retired in 1960, the company's name still acknowledges the respect of Lou Barbieri for his mentor.

Barbieri attributes the loyalty of the firm's clientele throughout the years to the standard of integrity set by Goodale. Goodale and Barbieri has long-standing clients, for example, whose property is managed without a written contract. Another source of satisfaction for Barbieri is the knowledge that he has worked to satisfy the interests of both buyers and sellers in complex property transactions.

In 1970 Donald K. Barbieri began working at the firm, becoming a full partner with his father in 1978. His graduate degree in urban planning led Goodale and Barbieri to undertake some federally subsidized housing developments in Spokane.

The first was the Cathedral Plaza Apartments, which the Department of Housing and Urban Development has used nationally as an example of a successful project. Before achieving this recognition the company had to overcome HUD's resistance to Lou Barbieri's idea that 15 percent of the apartments be rented at fair market value. Through this practice many neighborhood problems commonly associated with subsidized housing have been avoided.

In 1971 Lou Barbieri became chairman of the Expo committee that helped to determine the form of the Washington State Pavilion. What resulted was the opera house and convention center, which the state donated to the city after the fair.

Following Expo the Barbieris founded a hospitality division that in 1976 opened Cavanaugh's River Inn. This was followed by additional motor inns in Moscow and the Tri-Cities, with another due to open in Kalispell in 1986. Cavanaugh's Inn at the Park, which opened in 1982, has provided downtown Spokane with additional hotel capacity and convention space.

The operations manager for Barbieri Hospitality, Inc., is Tom Barbieri, Don's younger brother and a 1979 graduate of WSU's School of Hotel and Restaurant Management. Two other brothers are Mark Barbieri, with the commercial division, and Dick Barbieri, a Seattle lawyer and hospitality division secretary.

LEONARD'S MACHINE SHOP

Larry Heinen, the second-generation owner of Leonard's Machine Shop, enjoys the niche that his business occupies in the Spokane automotive engine rebuilding community. The four-man shop falls in between the large rebuilders and the one-man operations, and serves them both by handling the jobs that others either cannot or will not do.

The business was founded in 1947 by Larry's father, Leonard Heinen, who migrated to Spokane from North Dakota after Depression-era dust bowls made life on the plains intolerable. After working for others in Spokane as a welder, and helping the war effort in the shipyards, Leonard Heinen returned to Spokane to establish his automotive garage in a rented building at Hamilton and Mission. In 1959 he moved from those cramped quarters to a purchased building at North 2616 Hamilton.

When Leonard retired in 1974, his son Larry took over the business. He had graduated from Gonzaga Prep and studied law at Gonzaga University, but preferred his father's shop to other career choices. Larry saw the need for a shop that specialized in imported car and specialty engine rebuilding, and was the first in the industry to apply a more versatile industrial-style hone to automotive engine applications.

One result of this concentration on machine-shop-only service and subcontracting work for other mechanics was some disappointed customers from Leonard's era who still wanted the Heinens' personal service for general automotive repair. They are now gently redirected to garages that in turn supply Larry Heinen with engines to rebuild.

The engine rebuilding industry in Spokane is exceptionally large, supplying retailers in half a dozen or more western states with motors. Leonard's Machine Shop serves only local customers, though these often include the larger shops.

Employees for this trade are often trained at the area's community colleges, including Spokane Community College, where Larry Heinen serves on the advisory board for heavy equipment. Two of Larry's present employees are graduates of the SCC program, and two more, of whom one has since retired, have worked for both Leonard and Larry.

In addition to his commercial accounts, Larry also produces racing engines for Force Four Racing, an Indiana company that builds four-cylinder race cars for amateur race buffs. The publicly owned firm, of which Larry Heinen is vice-president, receives high-tech input from an electronics firm in which it recently acquired a stake.

Larry Heinen believes that the rebuilding industry is not only good for his shop but also provides important ecological benefits, because it reuses highly processed metal parts. This is part of the satisfaction that he receives in operating what he believes is Spokane's oldest family-owned automotive machine shop.

Leonard's Machine Shop has been rebuilding automobile engines from this North 2616 Hamilton location since 1959.

FARM CREDIT BANKS OF SPOKANE

When D.G. O'Shea arrived in March 1917 to establish the Federal Land Bank of Spokane, he found that sacks of unopened mail awaited him. Farmers' need for capital was pressing, and between the passage of the Act of Congress in 1916 and the selection of Spokane as headquarters for a four-state region, news of the federally chartered credit institution had spread. "Cheap Credit to Farmers" was the *Spokesman-Review's* banner headline for December 28, 1916.

O'Shea spent but four days in temporary quarters in the Federal Building (the present Riverside Avenue Post Office), before leasing fifth-floor space in the Columbia Building on First Street at Howard.

The bank quickly turned its attention to lending money to farmers through national farm loan associations—local cooperatives established by as few as ten farmers requesting as little as $20,000. First to be established was the Tobacco Valley National Farm Loan Association of Eureka, Montana, followed soon thereafter by a cooperative in Deer Park, Washington. In all, some 528 associations would be formed, 285 of those in 1917 alone. Before O'Shea's tenure as president ended in 1925, the Federal Land Bank had also built its first office building at Third Avenue and Monroe, the present BOF Lodge.

The purpose of the Federal Land Bank was to provide a stable source of long-term real estate credit for farmers, and to this end Congress had provided nine million dollars in total capitalization for the twelve regional banks. A need for increased short- and intermediate-term credit was also felt as American farmers sought to modernize equipment and increase productivity. For this purpose Congress established the Federal Intermediate Credit Banks in 1923 to discount loans for commercial banks. Ten years later Production Credit Associations, similar to the national farm loan associations, were created to further improve distribution of short-term credit to farmers and ranchers who needed it. More recently, loan eligibility was extended to producers and harvesters of aquatic products.

The last of the three separate institutions known collectively as the "Farm Credit Banks" to be established was the Bank for Cooperatives. This institution was founded in 1933 to lend money to agricultural cooperative associations, such as grain marketing and farm supply cooperatives. Subsequent legislation authorized the Bank for Cooperatives to serve rural utility cooperatives and provide international financial services to assist cooperatives in marketing agricultural products. One of the Spokane Bank for Cooperatives' first loans was relatively small, $10,000 at 3 percent interest, and went to the Spokane Valley Flower Growers' Association. Today the Farm Credit Banks make loans of all sizes, from as little as a few thousand dollars to sums topping $100 million.

Spokane's historical development has seen the Farm Credit Banks make the transition from federally capitalized financial institutions to privately financed lending cooperatives fully owned by their member borrowers. These banks currently serve nearly 57,000 farmers, ranchers, harvesters, and producers of aquatic products, and their cooperatives in the states of Alaska, Idaho, Montana, Oregon, and Washington.

The present Farm Credit Banks office building, built in 1982, was designed by the architectural firm of Walker, McGough, Foltz, Lyerla.

Spokane's first Federal Land Bank Building, constructed in 1923 at the corner of Third and Monroe streets, was occupied until 1934.

ABADAN, INC.

The firm that became Abadan, Inc., in the mid-1970s began as the Joe Y. Hollingsworth Company in 1951. Its owner sold alarm systems and Ozalid reproduction equipment, and operated a small reprographics shop at West 415 First Avenue. When Hollingsworth sold the business to John Wills two years later, the new owner naturally sought a new corporate name. He settled on "Abadan," after the name of the Iranian city where he was stationed during World War II. Wills was new to the reprographic trade, and he wanted a name that could accommodate other businesses besides blueprinting. In addition, the name put his firm at the top of most alphabetic lists.

During most of the 1950s no more than a half-dozen Abadan employees served the needs of Spokane and Inland Empire architects and engineers for blueprints and photostats and for equipment sales and service. Then, in a three-year period beginning in 1959, missile bases came to Spokane and Moses Lake. Suddenly, the firm grew from nine to thirty-eight employees and began round-the-clock operation.

Abadan's sudden growth in the early 1960s led to the decision to diversify its product lines within its principal market. The company became a complete source for architect and engineer supplies, including furniture, and continued to upgrade its reprographic services and equipment lines as older technologies became obsolete.

In 1964 Wills decided to become a stockbroker, and Lee Pennell, an Abadan employee since 1953, became manager of the business. He acquired ownership of the firm with his wife, Doris, in 1975.

The remodeled Abadan facility on First Avenue featured reprographic services, including blueprinting, in the mid-1950s.

An employee makes a photostat copy in the 1950s.

Growth remained modest during the early years, but picked up considerably with the real estate and building boom of the 1970s. Expansion demanded new quarters, and in 1973 all operations except reprographics were moved to a 5,000-square-foot location in the Vista Industrial Park. Abadan has since tripled its square footage at this site. In 1981 it moved its reprography shop from its former location on First Avenue to new quarters at West 304 Third Avenue.

Additional expansion also occurred outside Spokane. Stores were opened in Richland in 1975, Kennewick in 1978, and Yakima in 1979. WPPSS nuclear plant construction work helped to generate business in the Tri-Cities area, but the firm was not dependent upon it. It has since combined the two Tri-Cities stores into a larger facility at Richland, and has increased retail space at the location.

In 1973 the company added an office products division to its reprography and architect-engineer supply divisions. The firm recently became an authorized dealer of IBM typewriters—machines that complement its lines of photocopiers and other office equipment.

Abadan, Inc., has kept pace with changes in equipment that has made museum pieces of old photostat cameras and blueprinting machines. Now the company's officers and seventy-five employees look ahead to the electronic office with the same sense of challenge and determination to remain a leader in their field.

HOLLISTER-STIER

Robert Stier, M.D., and chemist Guy Hollister (left to right), founders of the local clinical laboratory that has become Hollister-Stier, the leading manufacturer of allergenic extracts in the United States.

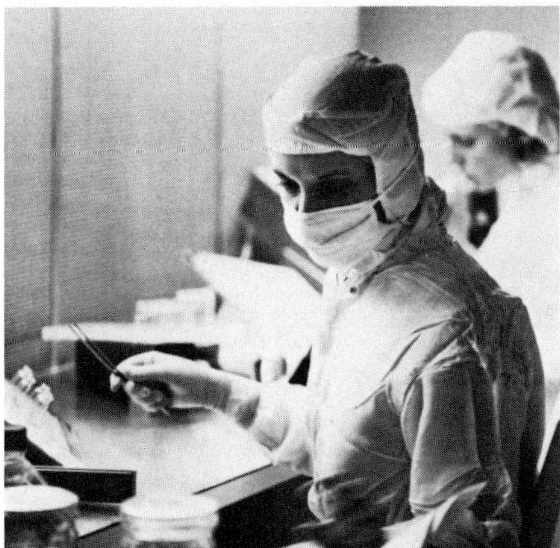

Allergen filling and testing at the company's Spokane facility.

It was shortly after World War I that Spokane chemist Guy Hollister sought relief from the hay fever that plagued him. After a chance encounter with a pollen-laden head of grass (he was mowing the lawn), Hollister decided to develop an extract for personal use. The project became the basis for the transformation of a local clinical laboratory into the leading manufacturer of allergenic extracts in the United States.

Hollister had begun the Spokane Clinical Laboratory in 1919 in the Old National Bank Building. But he soon felt the need for a pathologist, and advertised nationally. A New York resident, Dr. Robert F.E. Stier, moved to Spokane and became a partner. Together they developed grass, weed, and tree pollen extracts for diagnosing and treating hay fever. Hollister's first manufacturing location was a remodeled two-car garage at his home on Eighteenth Avenue.

In 1926 the partners renamed their business Hollister-Stier Laboratories. They hired their first full-time salesman in 1933, and by 1940 the firm's annual sales totaled $68,000. The company went nationwide during the 1940s, and by 1950 had sales of $472,000.

Hollister-Stier moved its fifteen-employee work force to new quarters at South 107 Division in 1951. Several additions would be made to the structure until the company built its present facility on a fifteen-acre site at North 3525 Regal in 1969. Plant size here has nearly tripled since then as sales grew from $3.6 million in 1970 to $22 million in 1983.

The founders of Hollister-Stier retired in 1961, three years after their company became a subsidiary of Cutter Laboratories of Berkeley, California. After 1968 the organization acquired additional depth with the establishment of separately organized sales and quality-assurance departments and the expansion of the research and development group.

In 1974 Cutter, and with it Hollister-Stier, was acquired by the German pharmaceutical giant, Bayer AG. Since then Hollister-Stier's production facilities have been consolidated in Spokane with branch laboratories only in Canada and other overseas locations. Since 1983 Hollister-Stier has operated as the Allergy Business Unit of the Miles Pharmaceuticals Group, which Bayer acquired in 1979 along with the parent organization, Miles Laboratories, Inc.

Hollister-Stier management attributes a large part of the firm's success to the quality of employees at all levels and a low rate of turnover. Approximately 210 people work for Hollister-Stier in Spokane, with 20 employed in Canada and another 50 in U.S. sales offices and distribution centers.

MILES LABORATORIES

Miles personnel at the opening of the fledgling firm's new office in Elkhart, Indiana, in 1892.

Much like the pioneering efforts of Guy Hollister and Robert Stier, the work of Dr. Franklin L. Miles of Elkhart, Indiana, provided the impetus for the development of Miles Laboratories. It all began with the doctor's theories that the human nervous system exerted more influence upon health than was generally acknowledged. His work led to the formulation of "Restorative Nervine" in the early 1880s. From its origins as the Dr. Miles Medical Co. in 1884, the firm grew to become a leading American manufacturer of pharmaceutical, chemical, and consumer products.

Dr. Miles had begun his marketing efforts with the aid of two local businessmen, but it was in collaboration with two later "co-founders," George E. Compton and Albert R. Beardsley, that the firm found its niche in the market and became profitable. Through his Grand Dispensary, founded in 1890, Miles developed a wide public following. Called "a medical evangelist" by one biographer, Miles disseminated medical tracts and pamphlets, almanacs, and calendars that both informed the public and advertised his products.

When Dr. Miles died in 1929 at the age of eighty-three, the business was just months away from a major breakthrough. Alka-Seltzer was the result of a company looking for a product, and of the technical prowess of a chemist who discovered how to make a tablet effervesce. After its introduction in 1931 it became Miles' mainstay, accounting for 73 percent of sales in 1953 and furnishing the profits that allowed the company to diversify.

During the 1950s Miles introduced new products like Bactine and One-A-Day vitamin supplements that gained broad consumer acceptance. Its Ames Division developed a line of diagnostic products that laid the basis for the firm's present position in medical analysis instrumentation. Through acquisition, such as the purchase of Dome Chemicals—a leading producer of dermatologicals—in 1959 Miles also obtained products used in life-science research and additional health-care products and chemicals.

By 1975 Miles had grown to more than $400 million in sales, with extensive overseas operations. Yet its management believed that further growth required resources the company alone could not provide, and sought a suitable merger partner. The suitor Miles chose was the German firm of Bayer AG, founded by synthetic dye maker Friedrich Bayer in 1863. The merger was completed in 1979. That same year the Dome Division, located at West Haven, Connecticut, was renamed Miles Pharmaceuticals, reflecting the attention to pharmaceuticals as a major growth area under the Bayer influence.

Bayer had acquired worldwide fame as a maker of aspirin after 1899. Its trademark, a cross within a circle, was introduced at this time. But the brand of aspirin sold in the United States under this name is owned by an unrelated company that bought Bayer's American affiliate from the U.S. government following confiscation during World War I.

Miles Pharmaceuticals in West Haven, Connecticut.

COWLES PUBLISHING COMPANY

From his modest beginnings as a minority shareholder in a bold nineteenth-century frontier newspaper venture, William H. Cowles constructed a business empire that, now in its third generation of family ownership, continues to play a major role in Spokane. In addition to publishing both Spokane daily newspapers, Cowles Publishing Company has four major subsidiaries: Western Farmer-Stockman Magazines; Inland Empire Paper Co.; KHQ, Inc.; and Pinnacle Productions International.

The story of the firm's origins goes back nearly to the beginning of Spokane's settlement by pioneers. The *Spokane Chronicle,* Cowles' evening newspaper, produced its inaugural edition in 1881 in competition with the *Spokan Falls Times.* Local newspaper lore has it that the *Chronicle* spearheaded the successful campaign to add a final "e" to Spokane's name.

It was ten years later that William H. Cowles (pronounced "Coles") entered the Spokane newspaper scene. By 1891 the town's competing newspapers had expanded from weeklies to dailies, and ownership of one—the morning *Spokane Falls Review*—had passed from local hands to the publishers of the Portland *Oregonian.* With its exclusive Spokane-area Associated Press franchise, the *Review* clearly held a competitive edge.

But its owners had not counted on the natural inclination of citizens to prefer a home-owned newspaper. It was this motive that prompted Horace T. Brown, a former owner of the *Review,* to seek the aid of three Chicago *Tribune* newspapermen, including William H. Cowles, to start a new morning paper. Their *Spokesman* was founded in 1890 in head-to-head competition with the *Review.* After three years of intense rivalry and continued financial losses on both sides, William H. Cowles and his Oregon competitors reached an accommodation. The *Spokesman* was silenced and Cowles became a 25-percent owner of the *Review.*

But Cowles had only to bide his time before acquiring the remaining 75-percent interest in the *Review.* If the financial drain of the three years of competition had not been enough to discourage his Portland partners, the depression of 1893 backed the *Oregonian's* owners nearly to the wall as advertising revenues plummeted and past-due accounts mounted. After a year, Cowles bought out two of his partners by agreeing to assume all of the *Review's* outstanding liabilities. The very next morning Cowles resurrected his original property and rechristened his newspaper the *Spokesman-Review.*

The *Spokesman-Review* did not turn a profit until 1898, four years after Cowles assumed complete control. But the former midwesterner had come to Spokane to stay, and he worked hard to make his paper successful. He also contributed greatly to making the *Spokesman-Review* influential, both in its home territory and in the nation as a whole. Cowles was a personal friend of Theodore Roosevelt and moved quite comfortably in national Republican Progressive Party political circles.

Under Cowles' leadership the *Spokesman-Review* became known for its strong editorial positions and its consistent support for Republican candidates for U.S. President—although it broke with the GOP in 1912 to support Teddy Roosevelt's Progressive candidacy. It favored Prohibition, but it also promoted some policies of such Democratic presidents as Woodrow Wilson and Franklin Roosevelt. Nationally, its greatest notoriety was achieved in 1948, when President Harry Truman, on tour in Washington State, remarked to reporters that "The Chicago *Tribune* and this paper (referring to the *Spokesman-Review*) are the worst in the United States. You've got just what you ought to have. You've got the worst Congress in the United States you've ever had. And the papers—this paper—are responsible for it." Coming from Harry Truman, this blast was interpreted by the newspaper as a compliment!

Spokane's evening daily, the *Chronicle,* was acquired by William H. Cowles in 1897. Originally Democratic in political orientation, it continued under Cowles' ownership as an independent paper with its own reporters, editors, and offices. This practice continued until 1983, when the editorial staffs of both papers were merged.

The Review Building in 1906.

William H. Cowles' two sons, Cheney and William H. Jr., joined their father in the newspaper business. Cheney Cowles was managing editor of the *Chronicle* from 1939 until 1943, when a military accident claimed his life. William H. Cowles, Jr., served first as business manager of the *Spokesman-Review,* then assumed responsibilities as publisher when his father died in 1946. The third generation of Cowles' family leadership is represented by William H. Cowles 3rd, president of Cowles Publishing and publisher of both papers, and by his brother, James P. Cowles, vice-president of Cowles Publishing.

The *Chronicle* and *Spokesman-Review* celebrated their respective centennials in 1981 and 1983. In late 1983 the papers occupied a new building constructed to harmonize with the landmark Review Building that was erected by the *Review's* Portland owners in 1890. This facility and the Chronicle Building (constructed in 1928) were expanded and restored in 1984. The new construction and renovation added needed space for Cowles Publishing Company and preserved two important pieces of Spokane's commercial and architectural history.

Though best-known for its newspapers, Cowles Publishing is today a diversified company with four major subsidiaries.

Located in the heart of a rich agricultural region, the newspapers moved early to meet the special information needs of farmers and stockgrowers. In 1915 Cowles acquired Northwest Farm Trio, Inc., its first subsidiary. The farm-publishing group (today called Western Farmer-Stockman Magazines) originally published three magazines—one each for growers in the states of Washington, Idaho, and Oregon. A fourth magazine, *Utah Farmer,* was added in 1950. Farm publishing operations were expanded again in 1963 when Montana Farmer-Stockman, Inc., was acquired. Continuing its commitment to agricultural publishing, Cowles acquired Arizona Farmer-Ranchman, Inc., in 1984.

As another natural extension of its publishing functions, Cowles owns and operates Inland Empire Paper Company, founded in 1911. Cowles acquired a major interest in the company during the Depression and gradually expanded its holdings until, in 1969, IEPC became a wholly owned subsidiary of the parent firm. Inland Empire Paper manufactures newsprint used by newspapers throughout the western United States.

An early twentieth-century view of the Spokane Chronicle *newsroom.*

With the rise of new technologies, Cowles Publishing soon recognized that its principal product was information—information that could be disseminated by means other than ink-on-paper. This recognition led to the acquisition of Cowles' broadcast arm, KHQ, Inc. KHQ was launched as a ten-watt AM radio station in 1922, making it the oldest continuously operated, licensed broadcast station in Washington and the first in Spokane. Cowles acquired KHQ in 1946 and has fostered its growth. In 1952 KHQ-TV went on the air as the first commercial television station in the Spokane area. KHQ-TV marked another "first" in 1955 when it broadcast the region's first full-color programming. In 1961 KHQ-FM was added to the company's radio operation. KHQ, Inc., has been an affiliate of the National Broadcasting Company since 1927. Call letters were changed in 1985 to KISC-FM and KLSN-AM.

As a logical extension of its broadcast activities, Cowles owns and operates Pinnacle Productions International, an audiovisual production company. Pinnacle was formed in 1983 when Cowles acquired the production facilities and other physical assets of Spokane Community Video. Pinnacle's state-of-the-art video equipment is housed in the Northwest's most modern production facility. The firm produces television commercials and provides production services for industrial, educational, and media companies throughout the United States and Western Canada.

DAVENPORT HOTEL

This 1956 view shows the majestic Davenport Hotel, which was designed by architect Kirtland K. Cutter in 1912.

Although the sign read "Davenport's Famous Waffle Foundry," the facility that stood behind it was a tent on the northeast corner of Sprague and Post streets erected by a relative newcomer to Spokane. In this way a young Louis Davenport, deprived of his restaurant job by the great fire of 1889, laid the groundwork for the true fame that he soon would earn.

Davenport promptly moved his ambitious food service to the ground floor of the Wilson and Clark building, erected in 1890 on the southwest corner of Sprague and Post. Gradually his operation expanded throughout the facility, and soon after the turn of the century extended into the adjacent Bellevue Hotel, built also in 1890 on the corner of Post and First. The restaurateur-cum-innkeeper named his hotel the Pennington and provided unity to the structures in 1904 by commissioning architect Kirtland K. Cutter to give them a mission-style facade.

The Hall of Doges brings the splendor of the Italian Renaissance to festive occasions at the Davenport Hotel.

Within the Pennington Hotel, Davenport unleashed the creative imagination of Cutter. Together, their eclectic tastes produced a room of Gothic inspiration, a Venetian-style Hall of Doges, and an oriental-flavored Pergola Promenade. And yet the best was still to come.

With the backing of investors, Davenport expended more than two million dollars to construct and furnish what was soon recognized as a world-class hotel. Designed in 1912 by Kirtland Cutter, the new twelve-story building occupied the remainder of the block bounded by Sprague and First, Post and Lincoln. Executed in red brick and sandstone with terra-cotta trim in Florentine style, the hotel opened for business on September 1, 1914.

Less than a year later the hotel and its president became the object of a glowing review published by the editor of *The Hotel Monthly.* John Willy described Louis Davenport as "a quiet, unassuming, earnest man in the prime of life who, . . . [after prospering in the restaurant business,] visioned the ideal hotel. This too has materialized, and more than materialized, for if ever building reflected man, the Davenport Hotel beams with the soul of Louis Davenport."

Nearly every commentator points to the grandeur of the Davenport lobby, which, according to Willy, "is an institution. We do not have words to adequately describe it." Cutter enhanced its effect by deliberately designing modest-size street entrances that preserve spaciousness for its appropriate place. Davenport decorated the Spanish

This 1907 photograph shows the Pergola Promenade dining room in the Pennington Hotel.

Renaissance-style lobby with Austrian rugs, walnut furniture, and an Italian-marble fountain. It was alive with plants, birds, and fish, and its hearth glowed with the warmth of an ever-present fire.

The philosophy of Louis Davenport was expressed in the motto, "Do more than the customer expects." But he tempered this approach to hospitality with instructions to his employees to refrain from providing services that guests did not want, and informed the public that because he paid his help well they would accept no gratuities.

The Davenport Hotel was designed with the needs of traveling salesmen in mind. For them large "sample rooms" were provided that were decorated in neutral colors to complement any display. For decades these rooms filled with manufacturers' representatives who brought fashions and other merchandise to Spokane by train to offer to retailers gathered from throughout the Inland Empire.

More famous guests polished the image of the Davenport as a special place to stay. The hotel hosted several presidents and former presidents as well as royalty, celebrities, and other prominent individuals. And the Davenport earned a special place in the hearts of countless Spokanites of every station whose various rites of passage were celebrated there.

The renown of the Davenport is such that local legend insists that the story of the arrival of a letter from Europe addressed to "The Davenport Hotel, U.S.A." is not apocryphal.

For more than thirty years Louis Davenport devoted body and soul to the hotel that bore his name. Entire owner of the property since 1928, Davenport sold the hotel and retired in 1945. He died in 1951 at the age of eighty-three.

The property has had many owners since 1945. In this time the hotel has seen both periods of neglect and moments of restoration. From 1954 until 1967 the Davenport operated as a part of the Western International Hotels chain (now Westin Hotels), during whose ownership an outdoor pool was built and a fourteenth floor added. The historic value of the hotel was recognized in 1975, when the Davenport was listed on the National Register of Historic Buildings.

Probably the lowest point in the Davenport's history was reached in the early 1970s, when 1,314 Spokane investors purchased more than $2.5 million in securities from owner Harlow Tucker in a bid to "save" the hotel. A year later, after the hotel entered receivership, Tucker pleaded guilty to securities fraud. The bondholders received nothing due to prior claims on the assets by the mortgage holder.

Since this time significant investments have been made to preserve the hotel and maintain its condition. From 1973 to 1979 the Davenport was operated by the hospitality unit of Lomas and Nettleton of Dallas, and from 1979 to 1983 by Warren Anderson and former Montana Governor Tim Babcock. In September 1983 Babcock acquired the hotel as sole owner and is attempting to secure financing to restore it to first-class condition, and return it to profitability.

Few can be found among the hotel's 200 employees, the city fathers, Spokanites of every age, and former guests, who do not pray fervently that the building and institution that embodies Louis Davenport's soul will survive its present moments of difficulty.

A Kirtland Cutter mission-style facade unites the separate three-story and two-story buildings that Davenport named the Pennington Hotel.

SPOKANE PUBLIC SCHOOLS

The foundations for Spokane's public school district were laid in 1875, when Indian missionary H.T. Cowley opened a school for the six white children living near the Spokane River falls. Two years later the pioneer community organized a school district and elected directors. Among them was Cowley, who rode on horseback to the Stevens County seat in Colville (Spokane County was not yet formed) to obtain his teaching certificate.

The annual report for 1875, prepared by C.F. Yeaton, showed a total of eleven children (aged four to twenty-one years) in the town, with an average daily attendance during the three-month school term of four. By the following year the number of children had increased to forty-seven, but no school was held because of war with Chief Joseph's Nez Percé Indians.

By 1878 school was conducted in the district's first building, a one-room frame structure situated on Lincoln Street between First and Second avenues. The county of Spokane was formed in 1879, and the city by the falls began its period of phenomenal growth two years later with the arrival of the Northern Pacific Railway. The impact on the schools was sudden. Within a decade six new buildings were constructed, aided in part by the unanimous passage in 1889 of the city's first school district levy.

Money became tight following the financial crisis of 1893. When district funds ran out in 1895-1896, the directors shortened the school term to eight and one-half months. Following the recession voters passed a new levy that provided students with free books and supplies, and instituted kindergarten classes in the public schools.

The preschool program lasted only until the end of the 1899-1900 school year, when growth in grades one through eight forced the kindergarten to yield its classroom space. It was restarted briefly during the 1940s and has been provided continuously since 1973.

Spokane's first class of high school seniors—seven members strong—graduated just in time in 1891 to witness the erection of South Central High School on the present Lewis and Clark site. The three-story edifice served high school students for only nineteen years until it was consumed in a fire of mysterious origin in 1910. During construction of the new school, students from both sides of the river attended the recently opened (1908) North Central High School, where classes were scheduled over a ten-period day.

The rapid growth of Spokane schools slowed during the mid-teens, with the school year 1918-1919 showing the first-ever drop in average daily attendance. By this time 15,000 children attended Spokane schools. Following World War I a moderate rate of growth resumed, until the school district's average daily attendance reached a pre-Depression peak of

A first-grade classroom in the early days of Grant Elementary School. The six-room brick school was built in 1899 at a cost of $15,000. In 1980 a new school opened on the Grant site.

Between 1980 and 1982 fifteen new elementary schools were completed as the culmination of a six-year project to replace buildings dating back to the turn of the century. Shown is Cooper Elementary School in northeast Spokane.

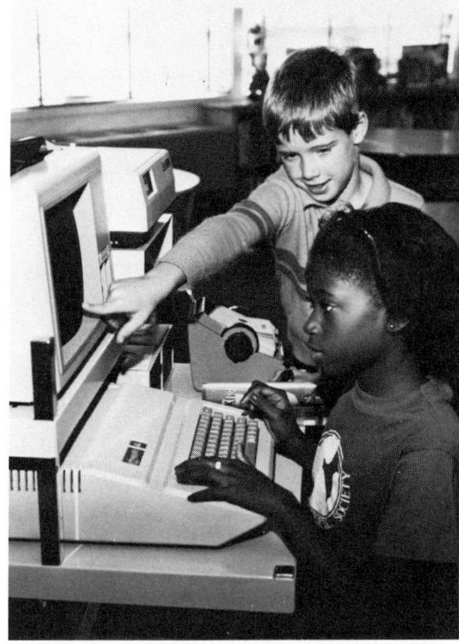

Spokane schools continue a tradition of excellence through carefully planned updating of curriculum and instructional activities and materials. By 1984 a computer education curriculum was in place in second grade through high school. Science courses are regularly reviewed and revised, and science requirements have been raised in recent years.

19,068 in 1930-1931.

In 1928 the school district opened two new junior high schools—Havermale and Libby—to provide a better transitional environment for young adolescents between elementary and high school. Provisions were also made for high-school-age students who had left school or were working. Spokane's Part-Time School served these youngsters from 1925 until 1932, when Joseph Jantsch became principal of Continuation High School. This facility's special mission was to make a high school education possible for those students who would not succeed in a regular high school environment. Jantsch's dedication to this task is commemorated in the successor school that bears his name.

Spokane's public schools provided classes for deaf children beginning in 1915, and ten years later assigned a teacher to provide instruction at the Shriners' crippled children's ward at St. Luke's Hospital. Today the Spokane district provides special education for severely retarded and handicapped children, and has worked to integrate the less severely handicapped into regular classroom environments.

This "mainstreaming" effort was facilitated by the completion in 1981 of an ambitious building program that replaced thirteen turn-of-the-century elementary schools with new structures at existing sites. The project featured a single-plan school adapted to each site that both sped construction and reduced costs. The buildings were designed with both educational needs and community use of school facilities in mind. A new district headquarters at North 200 Bernard Street was also completed in 1980 after a fire in 1979 destroyed the downtown building that the Washington Water Power Company had donated to the school district twenty years earlier.

The school district experienced strained relations with teachers during the 1970s over economic issues, class sizes, and problems associated with the mainstreaming of handicapped and learning-disabled children. A strike vote was defeated in 1975, but in 1979 Spokane teachers struck, delaying the opening of the school year for several days.

Since then the relations of the central administration and teachers have improved considerably, due in large measure to the conciliatory leadership of Dr. Gerald L. Hester, appointed superintendent in 1980. Support for Spokane's schools can also be seen among members of the community, both through voter approval of recent levy requests and through the willingness of approximately 1,000 volunteers to assist school personnel in classrooms and health rooms.

Spokane schools were "ahead of the game" in providing excellence in education, according to Dr. Hester. Even before the well-publicized report on the status of education, Spokane's junior high schools had increased requirements in science from one and one-half years to two years. And the district is strong in other academic areas as well.

Additional evidence of excellence can be seen in the 1982-1983 ranking of Sacajawea Junior High school as one of the top 152 secondary schools in the United States, and in the inclusion in 1984 of Dr. Hester in a list of the country's top 100 school managers.

Spokane public schools provide "a better education today than ever before," according to Dr. Hester, and to a more diverse student population. The 2,400-employee district serves approximately 27,000 students, about 9,000 fewer than the all-time enrollment peak reached in 1969-1970.

NORDSTROM, INC.

Spokane's Nordstrom store, located on Main Street at Post, following an expansion in 1977.

When sixteen-year-old John Nordstrom arrived in New York in the 1880s, an immigrant from the cold farmlands of northern Sweden, he had five dollars in his pocket, the last of a small inheritance from his father, and he carried with him one suit of clothes, the only one he had ever owned that wasn't homespun and handwoven. He couldn't speak a word of English.

At that moment the shoe business was the farthest thing from his mind. Yet, fifteen years later, after many trials and adventures, he founded a small shoe store in Seattle that, in time, would become one of the largest and most respected apparel and shoe stores in the nation.

Before embarking on this career Nordstrom had worked his way across the United States to California and then to Washington, earning his living as a miner and longshoreman, and at one point caring for the grounds, cow, and horse of a San Francisco architect. Drawn to the Klondike in 1897, he made a small fortune in gold. Two years later he returned to Seattle with $13,000, ready to settle down and marry.

Carl Wallin, a Seattle shoemaker he had met in Alaska, offered him a partnership in a shoe store. Nordstrom had invested some of his money in a few parcels of land in the city and eagerly accepted the opportunity to go into business. Together they opened their first store in 1901, with a twenty-foot frontage on Fourth and Pike streets. That first day John Nordstrom, the seasoned logger, miner, and Klondike gold panner who had never fitted a pair of shoes in his life (other than his own), nervously waited on the new venture's first customer. After rummaging through the back room, looking for the proper size, he made the store's first sale. Total receipts for the day came to $12.50.

The original Wallin and Nordstrom store, which opened for business in 1907, was located at 1422 Second Avenue in Seattle.

In the early years business was slow, but gradually it improved and the store grew. In 1929 Wallin sold his interest to Nordstrom, and a year later Nordstrom sold out to his sons, Elmer, Everett, and Lloyd. In the next thirty years they built the largest independent shoe chain west of the Mississippi, with twenty-seven stores.

At the end of 1963 the brothers purchased the Best's Apparel fashion specialty stores in downtown Seattle and Lloyd Center in Portland. Within six years they had a total of 420,000 square feet of space in several apparel stores.

In 1971 Nordstrom Best began to expand considerably its Seattle headquarters store and to establish a distribution center. To underwrite this expansion, the family offered Nordstrom Best's stock to the public for the first time.

During the next ten years management of the business was assumed by the third generation, and the firm continued to expand. In 1973 the company changed its name to Nordstrom. By the end of 1984 Nordstrom had thirty-nine stores in Washington, Alaska, Oregon, California, and Utah, with leased shoe departments operating in Hawaii.

Nordstrom entered the Spokane market during Expo in May 1974, with a store at West 724 Main. Remodeling and expansion in 1977 brought this facility to a total of 104,000 square feet.

PATRONS

The following individuals, companies, and organizations have made a valuable commitment to the quality of this publication. Windsor Publications and the Spokane Historic Preservation Foundation gratefully acknowledge their participation in *A View of the Falls: An Illustrated History of Spokane.*

Abadan, Inc.*
Action Women's Exchange
Dr. and Mrs. Richard E. Ahlquist, Jr.
Allied Safe & Vault Co., Inc.
Appleway Chevrolet*
Bastine, Coombs & Grabicki, P.S.
King F. Cole
Cominco American Incorporated
Cowles Publishing Company*
The Crescent*
Davenport Hotel*
EZ Loader Boat Trailers*
Farm Credit Banks of Spokane*
First National Bank in Spokane
Goodale and Barbieri*
Group Health of Spokane
R.A. Hanson Company, Inc.*
Ben and Dorothy Harney
The Haskins Company*
Hollister-Stier*
Home Environments
Inland Power & Light Company*
Fred S. James & Co.
Vern W. Johnson & Sons, Inc.*
Kaiser Aluminum & Chemical Corporation*
Kershaw's*
Key Tronic Corporation*
KOP Construction Co.
Lehman-Mills Associates
Leonard's Machine Shop*
McVay Brothers*
Metal Goods Service Centers
Miles Laboratories*
Millwood Furniture
Nordstrom, Inc.*
Northwest Architectural Company
Eunice O'Brien Realty
Olympus Industries, Inc.
R.A. Pearson Company*
Produce Supply Company*
Quality Inn Spokane House*
Riessen's-Evergreen Orthotic & Prosthetic Services, Inc.
Rosauers Supermarkets, Inc.
Sacred Heart Medical Center*
A.L. Skaar & Company, Inc.
Spokane Diesel Pump Repair Inc.
Spokane Public Schools*
Spokane Safe, Lock & Alarms
Spokane Steel Foundry and Spokane Metal Products/Division of Spokane Industries, Inc.*
Ticor Title Insurance
Washington Trust Bank*
Mr. and Mrs. R. Ronald Wells
Mr. and Mrs. Charles M. Williams

*Partners in Progress of *A View of the Falls: An Illustrated History of Spokane.* The histories of these companies and organizations appear in Chapter VIII, beginning on page 116.

SOURCES FOR FURTHER STUDY

There is room to mention only a fraction of the sources which went into the making of this book, so I'll emphasize those I found most helpful and/or those which seem to me would be valuable further reading.

All historians of Spokane start with N.W. Durham's three-volume *History of the City of Spokane and Spokane County, Washington, From Its Earliest Settlement to the Present Time* (S.J. Clark Publishing Co., 1912). Though lacking in objectivity, the work is a valuable source of raw material. Durham was an early editor of the *Spokesman-Review* and knew many of the people and events he writes about. Another valuable source of information is a chronicle called *Story of Spokane,* compiled by Orville Pratt, a one-time superintendent of Spokane schools. Pratt's notes about developments in Spokane up to the year 1948 are unpublished, but bound typescripts are available through the Spokane Public Libraries. A well-written (though somewhat out-of-date) regional history is George W. Fuller's *History of the Pacific Northwest, With Special Emphasis on the Inland Empire* (Alfred A. Knoff, 1948). The pattern of eastern Washington's development is told in a fascinating book by D.W. Meinig called *The Great Columbia Plain: A Historical Geography 1805-1910* (University of Washington, 1968).

Two Spokane historians, Jay J. Kalez and Roland Bond, have written several anecdotal histories of Spokane which are well worth reading. I used Kalez' *Saga of a Western Town, 1882-1972* (Lawton Publishing Co., 1972) and Bond's *Early Birds In The Northwest* (Enterprises Press, 1971). Another local historian who has contributed mightily to Spokane's small shelf of history is Wilfred Schoenberg, S.J. I consulted especially his *Gonzaga University* (published by Gonzaga University, 1963).

No one writes so authoritatively about the all-important mining history of the area as John Fahey. I used his *Inland Empire: D.C. Corbin and Spokane* (University of Washington Press, 1965) and *The Ballyhoo Bonanza: Charles Sweeney and the Idaho Mines* (University of Washington Press, 1971).

Barbara F. Cochran's *Exploring Spokane's Past* (Ye Galleon Press, 1979) is an excellent and accurate walking tour guide to Spokane's historic monuments. An interesting recent addition to Spokane history is Robert B. Hyslop's *Spokane Building Blocks* (available in manuscript at the Cheney Cowles Museum and elsewhere, 1983). Hyslop, an architect, traces the changes of buildings of every downtown address over the period of a century.

The story of the great flood which shaped so much of eastern Washington's landscape is clearly and succinctly told by Harlan J. Bretz in *Washington's Channeled Scablands* (Washington State Government publication, 1959). The discovery and significance of the Marmes archaeological dig is summarized in *The Oldest Man In America* (Harcourt, Brace, Jovanovich, 1970) by Ruth Kirk. Customs of this region's Indians are briefly described in *Children of the Sun: A History of the Spokane Indians* by David C. Wynecoop (published by the author, 1969) and *Manners and Customs of the Coeur d' Alene Indians* by Jerome Peltier (also published by the author, 1975). Two books which purportedly describe the Indian, but reflect much about whites, are *Nine Years with The Spokane Indians: The Diary of Elkanah Walker, 1838-1848,* compiled by Clifford M. Drury (Arthur H. Clark Co., 1976) and *Sketches of Indian Life In The Pacific Northwest* by Alexander Diomedi, S.J., (Ye Galleon Press, 1978), edited by Edmund J. Kowrach, S.J.

Three books are indispensable to understanding the area's Indian wars: the relevant chapters of *The Life of Isaac Ingalls Stevens,* written by his son, Hazard Stevens, who was with his father in these years and thus was an eyewitness (Houghton, Mifflin, 1901); *Ka-Mi-Akin* by A.J. Splawn (Caxton Printers, 1958), a flattering biography of a warrior to balance his treatment by most white historians; and B.J. Manring's *The Conquest of the Coeur d' Alenes, Spokanes and Palouses* (John W. Graham and Co., 1912), a balanced description of Colonel George Wright's campaign which cites original sources at length. Anyone seriously interested in local Indian history may want to consult the interviews and profiles in the collected papers of William F. Lewis, an attorney who early in this century did the community a great service by interviewing many Indians and pioneers.

Much of the early history of the city was fitted together bit by bit from diaries, letters and newspaper reminiscences to be found under pioneer names in the Cheney Cowles Museum. These are the sources of much of the information on Glover, Keats, Nosler and Campbell, to name a few. Though not published, these are accessible to anyone and make delightful reading. Aspects of Spokane's turn-of-the-century economics and social life are treated in *The Economic History of Spokane, Wa., 1881-1910,* a 1962 Gonzaga University doctoral thesis by William H. Kensel, and the *Age of Elegance* by Margaret Bean (Eastern Washington Historical Society, 1968).

One runs into a special problem in writing about the Cowles family. There are no family papers in the Cheney Cowles Museum and almost no articles have been written about them. The only book about the family, Ralph E. Dyar's *News For An Empire* (Caxton Press, 1952), was commissioned by the family. It is full of specific information, but of course is uncritical. I found useful a thesis at Washington State University, *The Spokesman-Review, 1883-1900, A Mirror To The History of Spokane* (1967) by Robert A. Henderson.

Two books on fascinating sideshows of the 1920s are *Rum Road To Spokane* (University of Montana, 1972) by Edmund Fahey, who tells his own story as a Prohibition-era supplier of liquor, and *Lionhead Lodge* by Lloyd Peters (Ye Galleon Press, 1976), a firsthand account about Spokane's brief flirtation with the movie business. Most of the handful of biographies of Bing Crosby briefly describe his Spokane boyhood, but the only book I found useful on the topic was his autobiography, *Call Me Lucky* (Simon and Schuster, 1953). The information about Crosby came mostly from interviews of those who knew him here, which I have treated at more length elsewhere (*Spokane Magazine,* December, 1977).

Even the contemporary newspapers shed little light on the conditions in Spokane during the Depression. A bibliography at Washington State University (Balzarini, S.E., "A Select List of Business and Other Records of the Depression Era in the WSU Libraries") provided some help, especially a 1937 summary of the city's participation in federal recovery programs called "City Progress Contest."

Descriptions of the Spokane home front during World War II were gleaned from contemporary newspaper accounts. Fairchild Air Force Base's official history, *1942-1982: Sentinel of the Pacific Northwest* by La Rine McGimpsey and Bill Harris was helpful with the background of that important part of the community. Stories of Spokane units and men overseas came from newspaper reports, interviews, and unit records. Notable in the last category is the four volumes of records on the 161st Infantry, Washington National Guard, compiled by William Bateman, historian of the unit.

The important question of the fifties and sixties, the Spokane economy, is well documented, though in sources not easily available. A series of reports called "Economic and Business Studies—State College of Washington," located in the Washington State University library, looks at many aspects of the Spokane economy in the decade following the war. Gonzaga University business students have contributed a series of invaluable theses concerning Spokane's economy and public attitudes toward it through the 1960s. Spokane Unlimited commissioned studies by the economic planning firms of Larry Smith, Inc. and EBASCO Services. The studies are available in the Spokane Main Branch library. The problem of sprawling suburbs is documented in any number of city and county reports, namely "Subdivision Activity, 1950-1957" (Spokane County Government, 1959). The change of form of government in 1960 is interestingly sketched in a handy volume of newspaper clippings called *The League of Women Voters Clipping and Materials Book, 1960,* which is available at Eastern Washington University. The politics of the mid-1960s are examined in a collection of papers called *Background Papers on Spokane* produced by the Eastern Washington University Community Services Institute (1967).

The seminal document of Expo '74, laying out the ground plan, is "Plan and Feasibility of Proposed Spokane Ecology Exposition" (Economics Research Associates, 1970). But there is no good comprehensive history of the Expo effort. The material in this book came almost entirely from newspaper clippings and interviews with Expo planners.

ACKNOWLEDGMENTS

I received a remarkable amount of help in writing this book. I want to thank Dr. Dale Stradling of Eastern Washington University for tutoring sessions on Spokane's geological history; Ruth Maston of EWU for her advice on Indian ethnology; and John Flett of the Spokane Indian Reservation, who could describe for me, from personal experience, Indian life both ancient and modern. Betty O'Laughlin of Spokane went to extraordinary lengths to help me gather some representative stories of Spokane's World War II veterans. Two people well versed in Spokane history, Dr. Michael K. Green and Nancy Gale Compau, read the manuscript for historical accuracy. My sister Sally applied the uncompromising eye of a college composition teacher to the manuscript.

Pam Schroeder of Windsor Publications has been a skilled and amiable editor, and I appreciate her help.

My mother, Frances Stimson, called upon friendships that include a good portion of the current Spokane population to find sources, facts, and photographs which were invaluable to the book.

My wife Kristine made too many contributions to list. To support just four lines of description, for example, she once worked from newspapers and city directories to chart every business operating on Riverside in the years of 1929 and 1934. She also conducted interviews, spent long hours in the library and, at the other end of the project, read and critiqued every page of the manuscript.

This book is written for William, Jr., and all the other juniors in Spokane. I could hardly have a higher hope for him and for all of them than that they might find Spokane as pleasant a place in which to grow up and live as I have.

William L. Stimson
Pullman, Washington

Kirtland Cutter bought a small cottage on the corner of Howard Street and Seventh Avenue and transformed it into his "Chalet Hohenstein," the first Swiss-style chalet in the U.S. (EWSHS)

INDEX